大展好書　好書大展
品嚐好書　冠群可期

大展好書　好書大展
品嘗好書　冠群可期

中英文對照武學(2)

李壽堂 編著　　張連友 校訂

42 式

太極拳

學與練

附VCD

大展出版社有限公司

42 式太極拳學與練
Study and Practice of 42-form Taiji Quan

作者　李壽堂

Writer　　Shoutang　Li

翻譯者　北美意源書社
　　　　孫慧敏　姜淑霞

Translator　　Huimin Sun, Yiyuan Martial Arts Books. North America

Shuxia Jiang, Yiyuan Martial Arts Books, North America

作者李壽堂和張連友的練功照

高玲華演示的42式太極拳

前　言

　　42式太極拳，是1989年中國武術院爲適應國際武術競賽需要，規範套路，組織專家在48式太極拳的基礎上編創成的國際武術太極拳競賽套路。有40個拳式，加上「起式」和「收式」共有42個拳勢動作，因此，亦稱爲42式太極拳。

　　42式太極拳以傳統楊氏太極拳爲範，吸收了陳、吳、孫等太極拳流派的代表性拳勢動作編排而成。因此，42式太極拳具有陳、楊、吳、孫四種不同風格。

　　42式太極拳以現代科學爲指導，根據生理學、人體結構平衡發展，較好地繼承了傳統太極拳輕鬆、柔和、圓活、自然、綿綿不斷的動作風格，體現了體鬆心靜、意領身隨、剛柔相濟的特點，並在此基礎上加大了難度和運動量，從而形成舒展、圓活、均衡全面、生動簡練的新套路。

　　42式太極拳與傳統太極拳相比，更具有科學性和時代性。

　　其一，它吸收了四大太極拳門派的代表性拳勢動作，規範了套路，爲各門派所接受，同時適應了國內外太極拳的競賽要求，便於太極拳的普及和推廣；

其二，它增加了左右拳勢的平衡，彌補了傳統套路的不足，更有利於健身；

其三，它以楊氏太極拳拳勢爲主，吸收了其他主要流派的代表性拳勢動作，不僅使套路內容豐富，而且更具有觀賞性，便於推廣普及；

其四，套路增加了難度和運動量，有利於太極拳的發展和競技。

太極拳屬於中國，更屬於世界。42式太極拳繼承了傳統，發展了傳統，優於傳統，它與時俱進，有利於太極拳走向世界、造福於全人類。

Preface

In order to standardize the forms to meet the needs of international Wushu competitions, masters and experts were grouped by the Chinese Association of Wushu to create the 42-form Taiji Quan in 1989, which was based on the Yang style 48-form. It consists of 40 movements plus the opening and closing form and becomes known as 42-form Taiji Quan.

The 42-form mainly comes from the Yang style of Taiji Quan, but it adopted signature techniques from the Chen, Wu and Sun styles as well, combining the different features of each of these four styles.

Guided by modern science especially physiology, 42-form puts emphasis on a balanced development of the human body. Its movements inherit all the characteristics of traditional Tai Chi: relax, soft, smooth, natural and continuous. It also fully embodies the Tai Chi spirits: relaxing the body, keeping internal stillness, feeling each movement, combining force with gentleness, etc. With the difficulty and the intensity being enhanced on this basis, the 42-forms came as a stretching, flexible, refined and all-round balanced new form.

In comparison with the traditional Taiji Quan, the 42-form has brought more scientific and modern components into the sport. A) It condensed the signature movements of the four major styles, standardized the routine and has been accepted by all the groups. Meanwhile, it remained fully compliant with the requirements of national and international competitions. B) Its enhanced the balance of exercising both sides of the body, eliminated the disadvantages of the original forms, and is therefore more beneficial to human body. C) Its movements were based mainly on Yang style and also combined those of other styles. Enriched in its content while becoming more appealing, it has gained much more popularity. D) The increased difficulty and intensity of the movements also propelled its development and usage in competitions.

Taiji Quan belongs to China as well as the whole world. The 42-form Taiji Quan inherited, developed, and surpassed the traditional forms. It continues to advance with the times, and it will surely benefit all the people in the world.

目　錄

Content

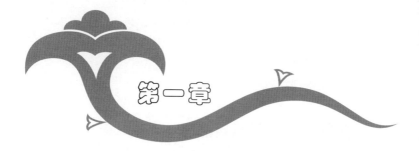

42式太極拳的運動特點及主要動作規格

Chapter 1 42-form Taiji Quan Features and Standards

第一節　運動特點及風格特點

Section 1　42-form Taiji Quan Key Features and Styles

一、運動特點

1. 體鬆心靜，呼吸自然

身體要舒鬆自然，思想要安靜集中，專心引導動作。呼吸要保持自然平穩，與動作和運動協調配合。不可勉強憋氣。

1. Key Points of Motions

(1) Relax the body and calm the mind，breathe naturally

Keep the body relaxed and natural while the mind is calm and focused on leading the movement. Keep the breath natural and even and coordinated with the movements；never deliberately hold a breath.

2. 動作走弧，虛實分明

動作順逆直橫，起落旋轉均要走弧形，分清虛實。

避免直來直去，生硬轉換，雙重僵滯。

(2) Move in curves and distinguish between the substantial and insubstantial

When moving forward or backward, up or down, or between the movements, move in curves and make substantial and insubstantial distinctly different. Avoid straight, rigid and sluggish motions.

3. 上下相隨，圓活完整

動作應手腳配合，上下協調，以腰為軸帶動四肢，周身完整一氣，圓活自然，不要上下脫節，支離割裂。

(3) Move the upper and the lower body coordinately

The limbs move coordinately with each other. The lower body coordinates with the upper body. The waist acts as the axel. The whole body moves as one smoothly and naturally. Do not move the limbs as individual.

4. 均勻連貫，銜接和順

動作之間要連貫銜接，勢斷勁不斷，不應中斷散亂；速度保持勻緩，不可忽快忽慢。發勁時，速度有所變化，但仍須前後連貫，連接順暢，周身完整。

(4) Keep the movements even, continuous, and connected smoothly

Movements should be connected smoothly, and the internal energy should flow without ever being interrupted or scattered, even if the motion comes to a pause. Keep the speed slow and even. When exerting force, change the speed a little bit, but keep the whole movement smooth and connected.

5. 輕靈沉著，發勁適當

運動輕靈而不飄浮，沉著平穩而不僵滯，外柔內實，綿綿不斷。發勁時，要發於腰腿，達於兩手；抖撒帶有彈性，做到柔中寓剛，剛柔相濟。

(5)Light but composed; forceful yet moderate

The movement should be light but not powerless, stable without being sluggish, even and continuous. The exterior seems soft; the interior is solid. The force should start from the waist and the legs and be delivered to the hands. The shaking of the sword or the body should be elastic, combining softness with force.

二、風格特點

心靜體鬆，動作柔和；
輕靈沉穩，意動勢隨；

虛實分明，剛柔相濟；

連綿不斷，勢正勁整；

兼收各式，融為一體；

轉接和順，中正安舒。

2. Key Styles of Movements

Keep calm and relaxed

Move lightly and stably

Motion follows the mind

Distinguish between the substantial and insubstantial

Unify the soft and hard

Act continuously, without pause

Posture correct, power focused

All styles of Tai Chi united as one

Connect the movements smoothly

Maintain the body upright and comfortable

第二節　42式太極拳的主要動作規格
Section 2　42-form Taiji Quan
Features and Standards

一、主要手型

1. 拳
五指蜷曲，拇指壓於食指、中指第二指節上。握拳不可太緊，拳面要平。

1. Hand Positions
(1) Fist(Quan)
Curl the fingers in, press the thumb against the second section of the index finger and middle finger. Do not hold the fist too tightly or too loosely.

2. 掌
五指自然舒展，掌心微合，虎口呈弧形。

(2) Palm(Zhang)
Stretch the five fingers naturally. The "Tiger Mouth" should form an arc. ("Tiger Mouth" is where the thumb and index finger are joined).

3. 勾

五指第一指節自然捏攏，屈腕。

(3) Hook(Gou)

Pinch the first sections of the five fingertips together naturally, bending the wrist down.

二、主要手法

(一)拳　法

1. 衝　拳

拳自腰立拳向前打出，高不過肩，低不過胸，力達拳面。

2. Hand Movements

- Fist movements

(1) Punch(Chong Quan)

Punch forward, moving the fist from the waist to shoulder height, turning it at the same time. The fist is not lower than the chest and not higher than the shoulder. Force should go to the fist.

2. 反衝拳

臂內旋，拳眼朝斜下，經耳旁斜向前方打出，高與頭平。

(2) Punch Reversely(Fan Chong Quan)

Rotate both arms inward, the eyes of the fists facing downward diagnolly. Punch forward, a little inclined, through the ears at the head height.

3. 栽 拳

拳自耳旁向前下方打出，拳面斜朝下，拳心朝內，高與膝平，臂自然伸直，力達拳面。

(3) Planting a Fist(Zhai Quan)

Punch downward (a little inclined) through the ears. The eye of the fist faces in and palm faces the body. After punching, the fists should be at the height of the knees. The arms stretch naturally. The force reaches the fist.

4. 搬 拳

屈臂俯拳，自異側而上，以肘關節為軸前臂翻至體前或體側，手臂呈弧形。

(4)Punch with the Back of a Fist (Ban Quan)

Bend the arm, palm facing down. Turn the forearm, pivoting on the elbow, punching from the other side of the body to the same side with the back of the fist, arm arched.

5. 撇 拳

一手握拳屈臂，拳心朝下，自異側向前上方翻臂撇打，拳心朝上，臂呈弧形。

(5) Throw a Fist (Pie Quan)

Clench the fist with one hand, arms arching and palm facing down. Punch to up-front from the other side, with the arm turning at the same time. After punching, the palm faces upward with arms arched.

6. 貫 拳

臂內旋，兩拳自下經兩側向前圈貫，與耳同高，拳眼斜朝下，兩臂呈弧形。單貫拳同此要求，拳略高於頭。

(6)Strike with Fists(Guan Quan)

Start with arms tucked in at either side of the body, bent, fists punching forward. The two fists move outwards so that both arms are outstretched on either side at ear level. When striking with a fist, the fist should be at the head level.

(二)掌 法

1. 單推掌

臂內旋，掌經耳旁向前立掌推出，掌指高不過眼，力達掌根。

- Palm Practice

(1) Push with a Hand(Dan Tui Zhang)

One palm at a time pushes out and forwards from the side of the head. Fingers should not be higher than the eyes. Deliver energy to the base of palm.

2. 雙推掌

兩掌自胸前同時向前推出，掌指朝上，寬不過肩，高不過眼，力達掌根。

(2) Push with Both Hands(Shuang Tui Zhang)

Push both palms forward from the chest, the fingers pointing upward. The palms apart should be not more than shoulder's width and the height not higher than the eyes. The force reaches the base of the palm.

3. 摟 掌

掌自異側經體前弧形下摟至膝外側，掌心朝下，掌指向前。

(3) Brush Hand(Lou Zhang)

Move one hand across from the other side of the body to the outside of the knee on the same side as the hand. The palm is facing downward, fingers pointing forward.

4. 攔 掌

掌經體側向上立掌向胸前攔，掌心向異側，掌指斜朝上。

(4)Blocking Hands(Lan Zhang)

Move palm from the opposite side of the body upward, and stop it in front of the chest. The palm is facing the opposite side, fingers pointing up.

5. 平分掌

屈臂，兩掌交叉於胸前，兩臂內旋，經面前弧形向左右分開，兩掌高與耳平，兩掌心朝外，掌指向上。

(5) Separate Palms Evenly(Ping Fen Zhang)

Bend both arms and place them crossed in an 'X' in front of the body. Turn palms outwards and separate arms out and sideways, stopping them when palms are at ear level. Palms are facing outward, fingers pointing.

6. 斜分掌

兩手交叉或相抱，斜向上下或前後分開。

(6) Separate Palms Diagonally(Xie Fen Zhang)

Make an "X" with both arms in front of the body. Separate them, one moving up and another moving down, or one forward

7. 雲 掌

兩手掌在體前上下交替呈立圓運轉為立雲掌;掌心朝上,在體前或體側呈平圓運轉為平雲掌。

(7) Cloud Hands(Yun Zhang)

Two palms draw large circles vertically and alternatively in front of the body. Or, draw circles horizontally in front of or at the side of the body.

8. 穿 掌

側掌或平掌沿體前、臂、腿穿伸,指尖與穿伸方向一致,力達指尖。

(8) Thrust Hand (Chuan Zhang)

Move a palm along the body, arm, and then leg. The thumb should point up, palm facing up or facing down, depending on the requirements. Deliver the energy to the fingertips.

9. 架 掌

手臂內旋,掌自下向前上架至頭側上方,臂呈弧形,掌心向外,掌高過頭。

(9) Upper Block with Palms〔Jia Zhang〕

Turn palm outward and move it up to the upper side of the head. The arm is arched.

10. 抱 掌

兩掌合抱，兩臂保持弧形，兩腋須留有空隙。

(10) Palm Holding〔Bao Zhang〕

Two palms are held together, and arms are maintained in an arc. All parts of the arms should remain a short distance from the body.

11. 挑 掌

側掌自下向上屈臂挑起，掌指朝上，指尖高不過肩，腋部須留有空隙。

(11) Lift a Palm〔Tiao Zhang〕

Lift a palm upward with arms arching, the fingers pointing upward at the height not higher than shoulders. There should be room left under the arm.

12. 開合手

兩手掌心相對，指尖向上，高與肩平，兩手平開與肩同寬為開手；兩手自左右向胸前合攏至與頭同寬為合手。

(12) Opening and Closing Hands (Kai He Shou)

Two palms face each other. Fingers point upward at the shoulder height. Moving hands apart to shoulder width is called Opening Hands (Kai Shou). And moving hands close to head width is called Closing Hands (He Shou).

13. 挒

臂呈弧形，單手或雙手向左（右）側後挒，臂須外旋或內旋，動作走弧線。

(13) Pulling with Two Hands (Lu)

Move one or both hands backward. to the left or the right side. as if pulling something back. Arms move in an arc.

14. 按

單掌或雙掌自上而下為下按，自後經下向前弧形推出為前按。

(14) Press (An)

Push one or both palms down. This is called "press down". Push one or both palms upward and forward. This is called "press forward".

(三)臂 法

1. 掤

屈臂呈弧形舉於體前，掌心向內，力達前臂外側。

- Arm Practice

(1) Forearm Push（Peng）

Bend the arm in front of the body. Push it outward and deliver the energy to the outside of the forearm.

2. 擠

一臂屈於胸前，另一手扶於屈臂手的腕部或前臂內側，兩臂同時前擠，臂要撐圓，高不過肩。

(2) Push with Arm and Hand（Ji）

Bend an arm in front of the body. Place the other hand on the wrist or inside of the forearm of the bent arm. Push both the arm and the hand forward at the same time. Arms are bent in a curve not higher than the shoulder.

3. 滾壓肘

前臂外旋向前下滾壓至體前，力達前臂外側。

(3) Rolling and Pressing with Forearm（Gun Ya Zhou）

Rotate the forearms outward in front of the body. force reaching the outside of the forearm.

三、主要步型

(一) 弓 步

1. 正弓步

前腿全腳著地，屈膝前弓，膝部不超過腳尖；另一腿自然伸直，腳尖裏扣斜前方約45°，兩腳橫向距離為10～20公分。

3. Foot Positions

- Bow Step (Gong Bu)

(1) Forward Bow Step (Zheng Gong Bu)

One foot takes a big step and the entire foot is planted on the ground, knee bent. The knee should not be over or past the toes. Straighten the other leg, toes pointing at about 45° outwards, in relation to the body. Feet are on two parallel lines, which distance is about 10 to 20 cm.

2. 側弓步

兩腳斜平行，一腿屈膝側弓，另一腿側向開撐，自然伸直。

(2) Aside Bow Step (Ce Gong Bu)

With toes on both feet pointing outward slightly, bend a knee and extend the other leg naturally.

（二）虛　步

一腿屈膝半蹲，全腳著地，腳尖斜向前；另一腿微屈，腳前掌或腳跟著地。

- Empty Step(Xu Bu)

Bend one knee with the whole foot planted on the ground, toes pointing a little outward. Bend the other knee slightly with either the palm or the heel of the foot on the ground.

（三）馬　步

1. 正馬步

腳開立下蹲，間距2～3腳寬，兩腳平行或外撇不超過30°，兩膝同腳尖方向一致，膝尖不可超過腳尖。

- Horse Step (Ma Bu)

（1）Even Horse Step(Zheng Ma Bu)

Squat with two feet being 40～60 cm apart. Keep the feet parallel or pointing outward less than 30°. Knees point to the same direction as the feet, but do not go beyond the feet.

2. 偏馬步

重心偏右或偏左，其餘要求與正馬步同。

（2）Lean Aside Horse Step(Pian Ma Bu)

Shift the weight to the right or to the left, and the rest is the same as Horse Step.

3. 半馬步

一腳腳尖向前，另一腳腳尖朝側，其餘要求與正馬步同。

(3) Half Horse Step(Ban Ma Bu)

One foot points forward and the toes of the other foot points outward. The rest is the same as Horse Step.

(四)仆 步

一腿全蹲，膝與腳尖稍外撇；另一腿自然平鋪伸直，接近地面，腳尖裏扣，兩腳全著地。

- Crouch Stance(Pu Bu)

Squat with one leg and knee and toes slightly pointing outwards. Extend the whole length of the other leg close to the ground, toes towards inside. The centre of gravity should be low and close to the ground. Both feet are fully placed on the ground.

(五)丁 步

一腿屈膝半蹲，重心在屈膝腿上；另一腿以腳前掌點地於支撐腳內側。

- T-Step(Ding Bu)

Bend one leg in a half squat. Put the weight on this leg.

The other forefoot is on the floor at the inside of the supporting foot.

（六）歇　步

兩腿交叉，屈膝全蹲，前腳腳尖外撇，全腳著地，後腳腳尖向前，腳跟離地，臀部接近腳跟。

- Lower Squat with Legs Crossing(Xie Bu)

Cross both legs and squat lower. The front foot points outward, all the sole on the floor. The behind foot points forward, the heel not touching the floor. Keep the buttock close to the heel.

（七）獨立步

一腿自然直立，另一腿屈膝提起，大腿高於水平。一種是小腿自然下垂，腳斜向前；另一種是膝外展，腳尖內扣上蹺。

- One Leg Stand(Du Li Bu)

One leg stands while the other one lifted with the knee bent in front of the body. The foot should be placed in front of the standing leg's knee.

（八）平行步

兩腳分開，腳尖朝前，屈膝下蹲或自然直立，兩脚外緣同肩寬。

- Parallel Step(Ping Xing Bu)

Place feet shoulder width apart, toes pointing forwards. Knees maybe be bent or straightened.

四、主要步法

1. 上 步

一腿支撐，另一腿提起經支撐腿內側向前上步，腳跟先著地，隨著重心前移，全腳著地。

4. Steps

(1) Forward Step(Shang Bu)

One leg supports the body. Lift the other foot from the inside of the supporting leg and move it forward, placing the heel to the floor first. As the weight is shifted, place the entire foot on the floor and the leg becomes the supporting leg.

2. 退 步

一腿支撐，另一腿經支撐腿內側退一步，腳前掌先著地，隨著重心後移，全腳著地。

(2) Backward Step(Tui Bu)

One leg supports the body. Lift the other foot from the inside of the supporting leg and move it backward, placing the heel to the floor first. As the weight is shifted, place the entire foot on the floor and the leg becomes the supporting leg.

3. 橫開步

一腿支撐，另一腳提起，以腳跟內側橫向擦地而出，隨著重心橫移，全腳著地。

(3) Sweep Aside(Heng Kai Bu)

Lift one leg and sweep the floor to the side with the inner part or the heel. Place all the sole on the floor when the weight moves to the side.

4. 側行步（雲手）

一腿支撐，另一腿提起側向開步，腳前掌先著地，隨著重心橫移，全腳著地逐漸過渡為支撐腿；另一腿提起，向支撐腿內側併步，仍須先以腳前掌著地，隨著重心橫移，全腳著地過渡為支撐腿，併步時兩腳間距為10～20公分。

(4) Side Steps(Ce Xing Bu)

One leg supports the body. Lift the other leg and move it outward to the side, and place forefoot to the floor first. As the weight shifted, place the entire foot on the floor and the leg becomes the supporting leg. Move the non-supporting foot beside the supporting foot, its forefoot touching the ground first. As the weight is shifted, place the entire foot on the floor and the leg becomes the supporting leg again. The two feet are 10–20 cm apart.

5. 擺步（搬攔捶）

一腿支撐，另一腿提起，小腿外旋，腳跟先著地，腳尖外擺而後全腳著地。

(5) Toes out Step(Bai Bu).

One leg supports the body. Lift the other leg and point the toes outward, and place the forefoot to the floor first. Then place the entire foot on the floor while toes pointing front and outward.

6. 扣　步

一腿支撐，另一腿提起，小腿內旋，腳跟先著地，腳尖內扣而後全腳著地。

(6) Toes in Step(Kou Bu)

Lift one leg and rotate the calf inward. Put the heel on the floor first with the toes pointing inward, then the whole sole.

7. 跟　步

重心前移，後腳向前跟進半步，腳前掌先著地，隨著重心後移，逐漸全腳著地。

(7) Follow Up Step(Gen Bu).

One foot takes a step forward, shifting the weight forward. The other foot follows half a step, and place the forefoot to the floor first. As the weight is shifted, place the entire foot on the floor, and the leg becomes the supporting leg.

8. 碾 步

以腳跟為軸，腳尖外撇或內扣；或以前腳掌為軸，腳跟外展。

(8) Pivoting Step(Nian Bu).

Pivot on a heel, moving the toes either inward or outward. One may also pivot on the forefoot, moving the heel either inward or outward.

五、主要腿法

1. 分 腳

支撐腿微屈，另一腿屈膝提起，然後小腿上擺，腿自然伸直，腳面展開，腳不低於腰部。

2. 蹬 腳

支撐腿微屈，另一腿屈膝提起，腳尖上蹺，以腳跟為力點蹬出，腿自然伸直，腳不得低於腰部。

3. 拍 腳

支撐腿微屈，另一腿腳面展平向上直擺，不低於腰部，以同側手迎拍腳面。

4. 擺蓮腳

支撐腿微屈，另一腿從異側經胸前向外做扇形擺動，擺幅不小於 135°，腳面展平，兩手在胸前依次迎拍腳面，須兩響。

5. Leg Movements

(1) Separate Legs (Fen Jiao)

Bend one leg and lift the other one with the knee bending. Then swing the low leg upward. Keep the leg and foot stretched naturally. The foot should be lifted not lower than the waist.

(2) Kicking with the Heels (Deng Jiao)

The supporting leg is bent. Lift the other knee and kick out with the heel. The leg is stretched naturally, the foot higher than the level of the waist.

(3) Patting a Foot (Pai Jiao)

Bend one leg and swing the other one upward not lower than the waist. Pat the swinging foot with the hand at the same side.

(4) Lotus Kick (Bai Lian Jiao)

Bend one leg and swing the other one past the chest, the

range of swing should be more than 135°. Two hands pat the swing foot in front of the chest alternatively, making two clapping sounds.

六、主要身型、身法和眼法

1. 頭——虛領頂勁，下頷微內收。

2. 頸——自然豎直，肌肉放鬆。

3. 肩——保持鬆沉。

4. 肘——自然下垂。

5. 胸——自然舒鬆，微內含。

6. 背——自然放鬆，舒展拔伸。

7. 腰——自然放鬆，不前挺，不後弓，以腰為軸帶動四肢。

8. 脊——保持自然伸直，不左右歪斜，前挺後弓。

9. 臀、胯——臀要下垂收斂，不可後凸；胯要鬆、縮、正，不可左右歪斜。

10. 膝——伸屈柔和自然，膝關節要與腳尖保持同向。

11. 眼——目視前方（前手）或動作的方向，做到精神貫注，意動勢隨，神態自然。

身法的總要求是：端正自然，不偏不倚，舒展大方，旋轉鬆活，不僵滯浮軟，不忽起忽落；動作要以腰為軸帶動四肢運動，完整貫穿。

在動作轉換時，眼與手法、步法、身法要協調配合，勢動神隨，神態自然。

6. Body and Eyes

(1)Head – Drawn up, chin is slightly tucked in.

(2)Neck – Upright, relax the muscles.

(3)Shoulder – Maintain relaxed and leveled.

(4)Elbow – Sunken naturally.

(5)Chest – Maintain natural, comfortable, depress slightly inward.

(6)Back – Naturally relaxed and stretched.

(7)Waist – Naturally relaxed, do not bend the pivot point of the body and limbs.

(8)Spine – Maintain upright naturally, do not lean in any direction.

(9)Buttocks and Hips – Pulled in; maintain upright hips.

(10)Knee – Extended or bent gently. Keep the Knee and toes in the same direction.

(11)Eyes – Eyes look at a hand placed in front or a moving hand. The spirit is focused. The mind and body unite. Facial expression is natural.

第二章

42式太極拳套路

Chapter 2　42-form Taiji Quan Spectrum

第一節　42式太極拳套路動作名稱
Section 1　42-form Taiji Quan Movements

第一組

1. 起 式
2. 右攬雀尾
3. 左單鞭
4. 提手
5. 白鶴亮翅
6. 摟膝拗步（二）
7. 撇身捶
8. 捋擠勢（二）
9. 進步搬攔捶
10. 如封似閉

第二組

11. 開合手
12. 右單鞭

13. 肘底捶

14. 轉身推掌（二）

15. 玉女穿梭（二）

16. 右左蹬腳（二）

17. 掩手肱捶

18. 野馬分鬃（二）

第三組

19. 雲手（三）

20. 獨立打虎

21. 右分腳

22. 雙峰貫耳

23. 左分腳

24. 轉身拍腳

25. 進步栽捶

26. 斜飛勢

27. 單鞭下勢

28. 金雞獨立（二）

29. 退步穿掌

第四組

30. 虛步壓掌

31. 獨立托掌

32. 馬步靠

33. 轉身大捋

34. 歇步擒打

35. 穿掌下勢

36. 上步七星

37. 退步跨虎

38. 轉身擺蓮

39. 彎弓射虎

40. 左攬雀尾

41. 十字手

42. 收式

Group 1

1. Opening

2. Grasp Bird's Tail – Right

3. Single Whip – Left

4. Lift Hand in Front of the Body

5. White Crane Spreads Wings

6. Brush Knees and Twist Steps（2）

7. Sidle and Punch

8. Pull and Press（2）

9. Step forward, Deflect, Parry and Punch

10. Withdraw and Push

Group 2

11. Opening and Closing Hands

12. Single Whip – Right

13. Fist under the Elbow

14. Turn Body and Push (2)

15. Fair Lady Works at Shuttles (2)

16. Kick with the Heel – Right and Left (2)

17. Hide and Roll Arm Punch

18. Splitting Wild Horse's Mane (2)

Group 3

19. Cloud Hands (3)

20. Stand on One Leg and Hit a Tiger

21. Separate Feet – Right

22. Strike Ears with Both Fists

23. Separate Feet – Left

24. Turn Around and Pat on the Foot

25. Step Forward and Punch Downward

26. Diagonal Flight

27. Single Whip and Push down the Body

28. Stands on One Leg (2)

29. Withdraw Step and Thrust Left Palm

第二章

42式太極拳套路

Group 4

30. Empty Step and Press Palm

31. Lift a Leg and a Palm

32. Left Shoulder Strikes with Horse Stance

33. Turn Body and Pull

34. Capture and Punch in low Squat with Crossing Legs

35. Thrust Palm and Push down the Body

36. Step up to Form the Seven Stars

37. Step Back to Ride a Tiger

38. Turn with Lotus Kick

39. Draw a Bow and Shoot the Tiger

40. Grasp Bird's Tail – Left

41. Cross Hands

42. Closing

第二節　42式太極拳的套路動作詳解

Section 2　42-form Taiji Quan Detail Explanation Step by Step

第一組

1. 起 式

（1）身體自然直立，兩腳併攏，頭頸端正，下頦內收，胸腹舒鬆，肩臂鬆垂，兩手輕貼大腿側，精神集中，呼吸自然，眼向前平視（圖2-1）。

Group 1

(1) Opening

a. Maintain a natural upright position. Place the feet together. Head and neck is upright; keep the chip in. Shoulders, hips, knees, chest, and abdomen have to be naturally relaxed; mind concentrated. Hands are at the sides of the body. Breathe naturally. Eyes look straight forward (Figure 2-1).

（2）左腳向左輕輕開步，兩腳相距與肩同寬，腳尖向前，上體保持原狀（圖2-2）。

b. Raise the left foot and step to the left, feet apart at shoulders width, toes pointing forward. The upper body is still upright. Eyes look ahead (Figure 2–2).

（３）兩手慢慢向前上平舉，與肩同高，手心向下，兩臂與肩同寬，肘微屈下垂（圖2-3）。

c. Raise both hands slowly to shoulder height and apart at shoulder width, palms facing down; sink the elbow (Figure 2–3).

（４）上體保持正直，兩腿緩緩屈膝半蹲，兩掌輕下按，落於腹前，掌、肘與膝相合，上下相應（圖2-4）。

d. Keep the upper body upright. Bend legs slowly to a half squat and push the palms down to the abdomen. The palms and

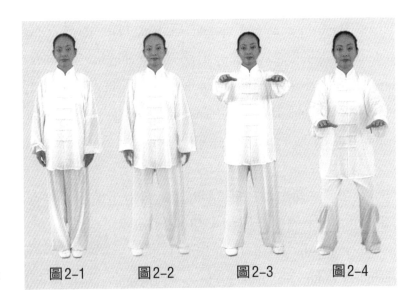

圖2-1　　　圖2-2　　　圖2-3　　　圖2-4

elbows correspond with knees. Eyes look ahead (Figure 2-4).

【要領】

（1）左開步時，腳跟先離地，做到點起；落地時，腳前掌先著地，為點落，而後再全腳著地。

（2）屈膝雙按掌時，上身保持正直，不可前俯後仰，按掌屈膝要協調一致，注意根節帶動梢節。

Key Points

（1）When the left foot stepping to the left, lift the left heel and place the forefoot down first, then the entire foot.

（2）When bending the knees and pushing down, keep the upper body upright; do not bow forward or lean backward. The hand push is coordinated with the bending of the knee. Ensure that the base leads the tip.

2. 右攬雀尾

（1）右腳尖外撇，同時上體微右轉。右臂上抬屈於胸前，手心向下；左手翻轉向右畫弧至右腹前，手心向上，與右手相對成抱球狀。重心移至右腿，左腳收於右腳內側，眼看右手（圖2-5）。

(2) Grasp Bird's Tail-Right

a. Swing the left toes outward and turn the upper body to the right slightly. The right arm is bent in front of the chest, palm facing down. The left hand follows the upper body to draw an arc to the lower right and stops under the right rip, corresponding with the right hand as if holding a ball. Palms are facing each other. Meanwhile, shift the weight onto the right leg and bring the left foot beside the right foot. Eyes look at the right hand (Figure 2–5).

（2）上體微右轉，左腳向左前方上一步，腳跟輕輕落地（圖2-6）。

b. Turn the upper body to the right slightly. The left foot steps to the left front with only the heel on the ground (Figure 2–6).

（3）上體左轉，重心前移，左腿屈膝前弓，右腿自然伸直成左弓步。同時，左臂向前向上出，高與肩平，手心向內，指尖向右；右手向下落於右胯旁，手心向下，指尖向前，兩臂微屈，眼看左前臂（圖2-7）。

c. Turn the upper body to the left. Shift the weight forward. Extend the right leg and bend the left knee to form a left Bow Step. At the same time, the left arm pushes outward. The left wrist and forearm are at shoulder height, palm facing in. The right hand draws an arc downward to the right side of the hip, palm facing down. Both elbows are bending. Eyes look at the left forearm (Figure 2-7).

（4）上體微左轉，右腳收至左腳內側。左臂內旋屈於左胸前，左手翻轉，手心向下，與胸同高，指尖向右；同時右臂外旋，右掌向左畫弧至左腹前，掌心向上，指尖向左，兩掌相對成抱球狀，眼看左掌（圖2-8）。

d. Turn the upper body to the left. Bring the right foot beside the left foot. Bend the left arm horizontally in the left front of the chest at shoulder height, palm facing down. The right hand follows the upper body to draw an arc to the lower right and stops at left side of the abdomen, palm facing up, fingers

圖2-5   圖2-6   圖2-7

pointing left. Both hands are corresponding as if holding a ball. Eyes look the left hand (Figure 2-8).

（5）上體繼續微左轉，帶動右腳向前方輕輕邁出一步，腳跟著地，眼看右前方（圖2-9）。

e. Continue to turn the upper body to the left. The right foot steps to the right front with only the heel on the ground. Eyes look at the right front (Figure 2-9).

（6）上體右轉，重心前移，右腿屈膝前弓，左腿自然伸直成右弓步。同時，右臂向前向上出，臂微屈，掌心向內，高與肩平；左掌向下落於左胯旁，掌心向下，指尖向前，眼看右前臂（圖2-10）。

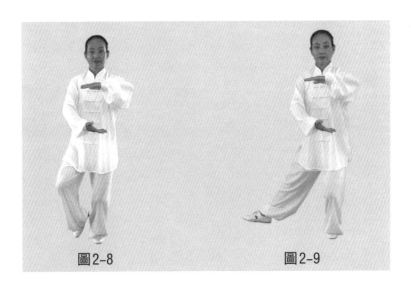

圖2-8　　　　　　　　圖2-9

f. Turn the upper body to the right. Shift the weight forward. Extend the left leg and bend the right knee to form a right Bow Step. At the same time, bend the arm and push it to the upper right at shoulder height, palm facing in. The left hand draws an arc downward to the outside of the left hip, palm facing down, fingers pointing forward. Eyes look at the right forearm (Figure 2-10).

（7）上體微右轉，帶動右掌前伸，掌心翻轉向下；同時，左掌翻轉向上，伸至右腕下方，眼看右手（圖2-11）。

g. Turn the upper body to the right slightly. Extend the right hand forward and turn it over to face down. Turn over the

圖2-10　　　　圖2-11

left hand to face up and extend it under the right wrist. Eyes look at the right hand (Figure 2–11).

（8）重心後移，上體微左轉，雙掌向下後弧線捋至腹前，眼隨右掌（圖2-12）。

h. Shift the weight backward. Turn the upper body to the left. Both hands draw arcs past abdomen to left back until they are in front of the abdomen. Eyes look at the right hand (Figure 2-12).

（9）右臂外旋屈肘橫於胸前，右掌心向內，指尖向左偏上；同時，左臂內旋，左掌心轉向外，掌指附於右腕內側（圖2-13）。

i. Rotate the right arm outward and bend it horizontally in front of the chest, palm facing in, fingers pointing the upper left. At the same time, rotate the left arm inward and turn the palm to face outward, fingers touching the inside of the right wrist (Figure 2-13).

（10）重心前移，右腿屈膝前弓，左腿自然伸直，成右弓步。兩掌同時向前擠出，兩臂撐圓，肘尖略低，眼看前方（圖2-14）。

j. Shift the weight forward. Bend the right knee and extend

the left leg to form a right Bow Step. Push both hands forward, arms rounded. Elbows are a little lower than the arms. Eyes are looking at the front (Figure 2–14).

（11）重心後移，上體微右轉，右腳尖上蹺。右臂外旋，右掌心翻轉向上，自前向右向後屈肘畫弧平移至右肩前，左掌仍附於右腕內側隨之畫平弧，眼看右手（圖2-15）。

k. Shift the weight backward. Turn the upper body to the right and raise the right toes. Rotate the right arm outward and turn the palm to face up. The right hand draws an arc to the right back, bending the arm in front of the right shoulder. The

圖2-12　　　圖2-13　　　圖2-14

left hand is still at the inside of the right wrist and draws an arc. Eyes look at the right hand (Figure 2–15).

（12）上體左轉，右腳尖內扣落地。右掌平旋內收，使掌心斜向上，眼看右手（圖2-16）。

l. Turn the upper body to the left. Swing the right toes inward and place them on the ground. Bring the right arm in and turn the palm to face upward diagonally. Eyes look at the right hand (Figure 2–16).

（13）上體微右轉，重心右移至右腿，左腳收至右腳內側，腳尖點地成丁步。同時，右臂內旋，右掌翻轉向右前方立掌按出，腕高與肩平，掌心向外，左掌隨之翻轉向內，指尖仍附於右腕側，眼看右手（圖2-17）。

m. Turn the upper body to the right slightly and shift the weight onto the right leg. Bring the left foot beside the right foot, with only the toes on the ground to form a T–Step. Meanwhile, rotate the right arm inward, turning the palm and pushing it to the right front, palm facing outward, fingers pointing up, wrist at shoulder level. Turn the left hand to face in, fingers still on the right wrist. Eyes look at the right hand (Figure 2–17).

【要領】

（1）掤、捋、擠、按四式動作要以腰帶臂，上下肢協調一致。

（2）本勢按式是單按掌，在按右掌時，左手指尖附於右腕處助力推按，右掌根與背形成一種對撐勁。

（3）上體要正直舒鬆，不可左右歪斜，前俯後仰。

（4）邁步、收腳落地要輕靈，均要點起點落，自然順逆。

Key Points

（1）The movement is led by the waist. Upper body is coordinated with the lower body.

（2）The press in this movement is using one hand. When pressing the right hand out, the left hand is on the right wrist

圖2-15　　　　　圖2-16　　　　　圖2-17

to help the force. Pull the back in the opposite direction.

(3) Keep the upper body upright; it should not lean back-ward or outward.

(4) When stepping forward or bringing the foot back, make it lightly and quickly. Always raise the heel or toes, and place the heel or toes first. Move naturally.

3. 左單鞭

（1）重心微下沉，左腳向左前方上一步，腳跟著地。右手由掌變勾手，勾尖朝下；左手隨上體右轉畫弧至面前，掌心向裏，眼看左手（圖2-18）。

(3) Single Whip–Left

a. Lower the weight. The left foot steps forward with only the heel touching the ground. The right hand turns into a hook and points downward. The left hand follows the body to draw an arc and stops in front of the face. The palm is facing inward. Eyes are looking at the left hand (Figure 2–18).

（2）上體左轉不停，重心前移，左腿屈膝前弓，右腿自然伸直，成左弓步。同時，左掌轉向前推出，掌心向前，腕與肩同高，眼看左手（圖2-19）。

b. Continue to turn the upper body to the left and shift the weight forward. Bend the left leg forward and extend the right leg naturally to form a left Bow Step. At the same time, the left hand pushes forward, palm facing forward. The wrist is at eye-level. Eyes look at the left hand (Figure 2-19).

【要領】

（1）勾手邁步時要鬆胯、沉氣，勾手向側後運勁。

（2）轉體前弓時，左臂要住，左手要內旋、左拉。

（3）弓步推掌時，要沉肩、墜肘、塌腕、落胯、氣沉，兩手對拉。

Key Points

（1）When the right hands turning into a hook and the left foot stepping forward, relax the hips; inhale through the abdomen. The hook pushes to the back right.

圖2-18   圖2-19

（2）When turning the body and forming the Bow Step, the left forearm pushes outward; rotate the left hand inward and push to the left.

（3）When pushing the left hand forward with the Bow Step, sink the shoulder, elbow, wrist and hip; breathe deeply. Push hands in opposite directions.

4. 提 手

（1）重心後坐，上體右轉，腰帶左腳內扣。左掌向右平擺畫弧，眼看左手（圖2-20）。

（4）Lift Hand in Front of the Body

a. Shift the weight backward and turn the upper body to the right, leading the left toes swung inward. The left hand draws an arc to the left. Eyes look at the left hand（Figure 2-20）.

（2）重心移於左腿，右勾手變掌，兩掌同時向左平帶（圖2-21）。

b. Shift the weight onto the left leg. The right hand changes from the hook into an open palm. Move both hands to the left simultaneously（Figure 2-21）.

（3）上體微右轉，右腳提起，腳跟落地，腳尖上蹺，成右虛步。同時，右掌成側立掌舉於體前，指尖高與眉齊；左臂屈收，左手也成側立掌合於右肘內側，眼看右掌（圖2-22）。

c. Turn the upper body to the right slightly. Lift the right toes with the heel still on the ground to form a right Empty Step. Meanwhile, raise the right hand in front of the body, the fingertips at the eyebrow-height, palm facing the left, fingers pointing upward. Bring the left hand inside of the right elbow, palm facing right, fingers pointing upward. Eyes look at the right hand (Figure 2-22).

【要領】

（1）虛步方向偏右30°，即起勢方向偏右。

（2）重心先後移，再轉體擺臂，右勾手變掌。

圖2-20　　　　圖2-21　　　　圖2-22

（3）重心左移提右腳與轉體向左平帶臂要協調一致，不可支離割裂。

（4）右腳跟落地與兩臂在體前相合要同時完成，兩手臂要有一種相合前送的合勁。

Key Points

（1）The direction of the raising hand is 30° to the right of the Opening form.

（2）Shift the weight backward first, then turn the upper body and swing the arm; change the right hand from the hook into an open palm.

（3）The shifting of the weight and the leading of the arms by the body are coordinated; don't complete them individually.

（4）The right foot falls to the ground at the same time as the two arms are raised in front of the body. Both hands are intended to push together and forward, without obvious action.

5. 白鶴亮翅

（1）上體左轉，右腳稍後撤，腳尖內扣。同時，兩手向左下方畫弧，再翻轉抱於左胸前，左手在上，手心向下；右手在下，手心向上，兩臂微屈成弧形，眼看左手（圖2-23）。

（5）White Crane Spreads Wings

a. Turn the upper body to the left. Move the right foot

slightly backward, and swing toes inward. Meanwhile, move both hands to the lower left and turn over to form an "X" at the left side of the body. The left hand is above the right one. The left hand is facing downward, the right one facing upward. Arms are arched. Eyes look at the left hand (Figure 2–23).

（2）重心右移，上體右轉，兩手邊合邊舉至右肩前，眼看右手（圖2-24）。

b. Shift the weight to the right. Turn the upper body to the right. Move both hands in front of the right shoulder. Eyes look at the right hand (Figure 2–24).

（3）上體微左轉，左腳稍向內收，腳尖點地成左

圖2-23　　　　圖2-24

虛步。同時，兩手右上左下畫弧分開，右掌提至右額前，掌心向左，指尖向上；左掌下按於左胯旁，掌心向下，指尖向前，兩臂保持弧形，眼看前方（圖2- 25 ）。

c. Turn the upper body to the left slightly. The left foot steps backward slightly, with only the toes touching the ground to form an "Empty Step". Meanwhile, move the right hand over the right side of the forehead, palm facing left, fingers pointing up; move the left palm down slowly to the side of the left hip, palm facing down, fingertips pointing forward. The arms are arched. Eyes look ahead (Figure 2–25).

【要領】

（1）上體左轉、扣腳、兩掌抱球這幾個動作要周身協調配合，運轉和順。

（2）上體右轉，向右上帶臂，再向左轉體，左掌下按，右掌上提，下肢成虛步時，腰鬆，氣要沉，頂頭，斂臀。上體始終保持正直，勿左右搖擺，塌腰凸臀。

（3）全部動作中，腰部旋轉要自然連貫，以腰帶動四肢。兩臂始終走弧線成弧形。保持周身勁整。

Key Points

（1）The upper body turns in coordination with the moving hands and feet. Motions are connected smoothly.

（2）Turn the upper body to the right to lead the right arm moving upward. Turn the upper body to the left to lead the left hand pressing downward. When raising the right hand and forming the Empty Step, relax the waist; inhale to the abdomen; draw the head up; pull in the buttocks; maintain an upright upper body; do not bend forwards or backwards;

（3）In the entire movement, turn the waist smoothly and naturally; waist leads the limbs. Move the arms in arcs. Move the entire body as one.

6. 摟膝拗步（二）

（1）上體微左轉，右手隨之向左畫弧，自頭前下落，眼看右手（圖2-26）。

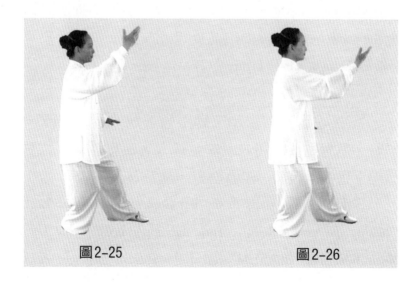

圖2-25　　　　　圖2-26

(6) Brush Knees and Twist Steps(2)

a. Turn the upper body to the left slightly. The right hand follows the body to draw an arc to the left and fall in front of the head. Eyes look at the right hand (Figure 2-26).

（2）上體右轉，隨之右手向下向右向上畫弧至右前方，高與頭平，手心斜向上；同時，左手向上向右向下畫弧至右肋旁，手心向下。左腳同時收至右腳內側，眼看右手（圖2-27）。

b. Turn the upper body to the right. The right hand draws an arc downward, then to the right, then upward to stop in the right front of the head, palm facing upward diagonally. Meanwhile, raise the left hand upward, then to the right, then downward and stop it beside the right ribs, palm facing down. At the same time, place the left foot beside the right foot. Eyes look at the right hand (Figure 2-27).

（3）左腳向前上步，腳跟輕著地，上體左轉。同時，右臂屈肘，將右手收至耳旁，掌心斜向前；左手向下畫弧至腹前，眼看前方（圖2-28）。

c. The left foot steps to the left front, with only the heel touching the ground lightly. Turn the upper body to the left. Meanwhile, bend the right arm at the side of the right ear, palm facing forward diagonally, fingers pointing up. Move the left hand in front of the abdomen. Eyes look at the front (Figure 2-28).

（4）重心前移，左腿屈膝前弓，右腿自然伸直，成左弓步。同時，上體左轉不停，將右掌變立掌向前推出，指尖高與鼻平；左手由左膝前摟過，按於左胯旁，眼看左手（圖2-29）。

d. Shift the weight forward. Bend the left knee and extend the right leg to form a left Bow Step. Meanwhile, continue to turn the upper body to the left; push the right palm forward, fingertips at the nose level. Move the left hand around the left knee to the outside of the left hip. Eyes look at the left hand

圖2-27　　　圖2-28　　　　圖2-29

(Figure 2-29).

（5）重心稍後移，左腳尖外撇，上體左轉。右手隨之向左畫弧，左手略前送外旋將手翻轉，眼隨右手（圖2-30）。

e. Shift the weight backward. Swing the left toes outward. Turn the upper body to the left. The right hand draws an arc to the left. Move the left hand forward and outward to turn it over. Eyes look at the right hand (Figure 2-30).

（6）上體左轉不停，左手向左向上畫弧，舉至身體左前方，高與頭平，手心斜向上；同時，右手擺至左肋旁，手心向下。右腳收至左腳內側，眼看左手（圖2-31）。

f. Continue to turn the upper body to the left. The left hand draws an arc to the left then upward and stops in the left front at the body, palm facing upward diagonally. Meanwhile, move the right hand beside the left ribs, palm facing down. At the same time, place the right foot beside the left foot. Eyes look at the left hand (Figure 2-31).

（7）右腳向前邁步，腳跟輕著地，上體右轉。同時，左臂屈肘，將左手收至耳旁，手心斜向前；右手向右向下畫弧至腹前，眼看前方（圖2-32）。

g. The right leg steps forward, with only the heel touching the ground lightly. Turn the upper body to the right. Meanwhile, bend the left arm at the side of the right ear, palm facing forward diagonally, fingers pointing up. Move the right hand in front of the abdomen. Eyes look at the front (Figure 2-32).

（8）上體右轉不停至正前，重心前移，右腿屈膝前弓，左腿自然伸直成右弓步。同時，左手成立掌向前推出，指尖高與鼻平；右手由右膝前摟過，按於右胯旁，眼看左手（圖2-33）。

h. Continue to turn the upper body to face the front. Shift

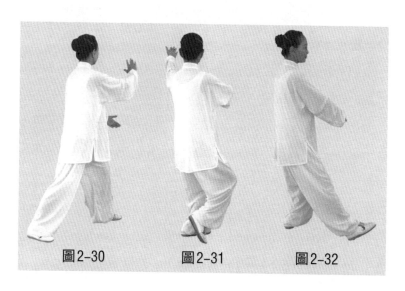

圖2-30　　圖2-31　　圖2-32

the weight forward. Bend the right knee and extend the left leg to form a right Bow Step. Meanwhile, push the left palm forward, fingertips at the nose level. Move the right hand around the right knee to the outside of the right hip. Eyes look at the left hand (Figure 2-33).

【要領】

（1）兩臂運轉要以腰為軸，全身協調一致。

（2）弓步時，前腳尖向正前，兩腳橫向距離約20公分。

（3）收腳、舉臂，上體要舒鬆正直，鬆胯斂臀，不可左右歪斜。

（4）弓步、摟掌、推掌要協調一致，同時完成，上體微前傾。推掌側肩部要前送，勁達掌根。

Key Points

（1）The waist is acting as an axel; the whole body moves in coordination with it.

（2）When making the Bow Step, the toes of the bowed leg is pointing forward; feet are on standing two parallel lines which is about 20 cm apart.

（3）When bringing in the foot and raising the arm, keep the upper body upright and comfortable; sink the hips; pull in the buttocks; do not lean the body to the right or left.

(4) Push the hand in coordination with the Bow Stepping, and the other hand pushes at the same time. Bend the upper body forward slightly. Deliver the energy to the base of the pushing hand.

7. 撇身捶

（1）重心稍後移，右腳尖外撇，上體右轉。左手向左前伸展，手心向下；右前臂外旋，右手向右後方畫弧分開，眼看左手（圖2-34）。

(7) Sidle and Punch

a. Shift the weight backward. Turn the upper body to the right and swing the right toes outward. Extend the left hand to the left front, palm facing downward. Move the right forearm outward and the right hand draws an arc to the back right. Look

圖2-33   圖2-34

at the left hand (Figure 2-34).

（2）左腳收於右腳內側。同時，左手握拳，臂內旋下落於小腹前，拳心向內，拳眼向右；右手向上，舉於右額上方，手心向上，眼看前方（圖2-35）。

b. Bring the left foot in and place it beside the right foot. Meanwhile, turn the left hand into a fist, and it falls in front of the abdomen, palm facing the body, the eye of the fist facing the right. Move the right hand upward and stop it above the right forehead, palm facing upward. Look at the front(Figure 2-35).

（3）上體微右轉，左腳向左前方上步，腳跟著地。左拳上舉至面前，右掌下落於左前臂內側，手心向下，眼看左拳（圖2-36）。

c. Turn the upper body to the right slightly. The left foot steps to the left front, with the heel touching the ground. Raise the left fist in front of the face. The right palm falls to the inside of the left forearm, palm facing downward. Look at the left fist (Figure 2-36).

（4）上體左轉，重心前移，左腿屈膝前弓，右腿自然伸直，成左弓步。同時，左拳翻轉向左前方撇打，拳心斜向上，高與頭平；右手仍附於左前臂內側，眼看左拳（圖2-37）。

d. Turn the upper body to the left. Shift the weight forward. Bend the left knee forward and extend the right leg naturally to form a left Bow Step. Meanwhile, the left fist punches to the left front with the back of the fist at the head height, palm facing upward. The right hand falls down to the inside of the left elbow. Eyes look at the left fist (Figure 2-37).

【要領】

（1）撇捶要轉身帶臂，以左肘關節為軸外旋。

（2）撇打時，右手要附於靠近左肘彎一側，力達拳面。

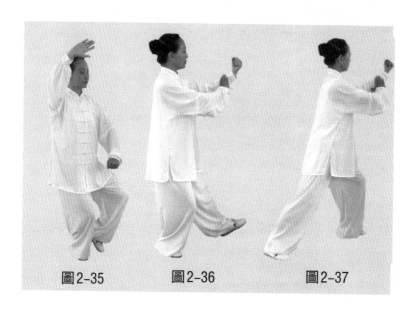

圖2-35　　　　圖2-36　　　　圖2-37

（3）撇打捶方向與弓步方向一致，斜向左前方30°。

Key Points

（1）When punching, turn the body to lead the arm outward; the left elbow is acting as an axel.

（2）The right hand is on the inside of the left elbow. Deliver the energy to the back of the fist.

（3）The direction of the punching is 30° to the left front.

8. 捋擠勢（二）

（1）重心稍後移，左腳尖內扣，上體右轉。左拳變為掌，右掌向右畫一平弧，隨即收於左前臂內側（圖2-38）。

(8) Pull and Press (2)

a. Shift the weight backward. Swing the left toes inward. Turn the upper body to the right. Change the left hand from the fist into an open palm and move it to the right first, then stop it inside of the left forearm (Figure 2-38).

（2）重心前移，上體繼續右轉。右掌由左向右前方畫弧平抹，掌心斜向下；左掌落於右肘內側下方，掌心斜向上，眼看右手（圖2-39）。

b. Shift the weight forward. Turn the upper body to the

right. The right hand draws an arc to the front right, palm facing downward diagonally. The left hand falls downward to the inside of the left elbow, palm facing up diagonally. Look at the right hand（Figure 2-39）.

（3）上體微左轉，兩掌自前同時向下向後将，左掌将至左胯旁，右掌将至腹前。右腳收至左腳內側，眼看右前方（圖2-40）。

c. Turn the upper body to the left slightly. both hands draw arcs past abdomen to left back until the left hand is beside the left hip and the right hand in front of the abdomen. Eyes look at the front（Figure 2-40）.

圖2-38　　　　圖2-39　　　　圖2-40

（4）上體右轉，右腳向右前方上步，腳跟著地。同時，左前臂內旋，右前臂外旋，兩手翻轉屈臂上舉，收於胸前，手心相對，眼看前方（圖2-41）。

d. Turn the upper body to the right. The right foot steps to the right front with only the heel on the ground. At the same time, rotate the left forearm inward, the right one outward. Turn both hands over and bring them in front of the chest, palm facing each other. Eyes look at the front（Figure 2-41）.

（5）重心前移，右腿屈膝，左腿自然伸直，成右弓步。兩臂同時向前擠出，兩臂撐圓；左掌指貼於右腕內側，掌心向外，指尖斜向上；右掌心向內，指尖向左，高與肩平，眼看右手（圖2-42）。

e. Shift the weight forward. Extend the left leg and bend the right knee to form a right Bow Step. Push both hands forward; arms are rounded; elbows are a little lower than the arms. The left hand is still on the inside of the right wrist, palm facing outward, fingers pointing up diagonally. The right palm is facing in, fingers pointing left at shoulder level. Eyes are looking at the right hand（Figure 2-42）.

（6）重心後移，右腳尖內扣，上體左轉。右掌翻轉向上，左掌畫一小弧從右前臂上方穿出（圖2-43）。

f. Shift the weight backward. Swing the right toes inward. Turn the upper body to the left. Turn the right hand over. Move the left hand forward over the left forearm (Figure 2–43).

（7）重心前移，上體繼續左轉。左掌自右向左前方畫弧平抹，掌心斜向下；右掌收於左肘內側下方，掌心斜向上，眼看左手（圖2-44）。

g. Shift the weight forward. Turn the upper body to the left. The left hand draws an arc to the front left, palm facing downward diagonally. The right hand falls down to the inside of the right elbow, palm facing up diagonally. Look at the left hand (Figure 2–44).

圖2-41　　　　圖2-42　　　　圖2-43

（8）上體稍右轉，兩掌自前同時向下向後捋，右掌捋至右胯旁，左掌捋至腹前。同時，左腳收至右腳內側，眼看左前方（圖2-45）。

h. Turn the upper body to the right slightly. Both hands draw arcs past abdomen to lower back until the right hand is beside the right hip and the left hand in front of the abdomen. Eyes look at the left front（Figure 2-45）.

（9）上體左轉，左腳向左前方上一步，腳跟著地。同時，右前臂內旋，左前臂上旋，兩手翻轉屈臂上舉收於胸前，手心相對，眼看前方（圖2-46）。

i. Turn the upper body to the left. The left foot steps to the left front with only the heel on the ground. At the same time,

圖2-44　　　　　　圖2-45

rotate the right forearm inward, the left one outward. Turn both hands over and bring them in front of the chest, palm facing each other. Eyes look at the front (Figure 2–46).

（10）重心前移，左腿屈膝前弓，右腿自然伸直，成左弓步。兩臂一同向前擠出，兩臂撐圓，右掌指貼於左腕內側，掌心向外，指尖斜向上；左掌心向內，指尖向右，高與肩平，眼看左掌（圖2-47）。

j. Shift the weight forward. Extend the right leg and bend the left knee to form a left Bow Step. Push both hands forward; arms are rounded; elbows are a little lower than the arms. The right hand is still on the inside of the left wrist, palm facing outward, fingers pointing up diagonally. The left palm is facing

圖2-46　　　　　　　圖2-47

in, fingers pointing the left at shoulder level. Eyes are looking at the left hand (Figure 2–47).

【要領】

（1）完成此勢要以腰帶臂，轉體進身，保持上體中正，頭上領，不要搖頭。

（2）後坐蹺腳與後手畫弧，弓步與穿掌，捋掌與收腳，出腳與臂，弓步與前擠，這一組動作要上下肢協調配合，不可分解。

Key Points

（1）The movement is led by the waist. When turning the body or moving forward, keep upper body upright; draw the head up; do not shake the head.

（2）Shift the weight backward in coordination with the drawing of the arc. Bow Step is coordinated with moving the hand forward. Bring the foot back is coordinated with pulling the hands back. Push is coordinated with stepping forward. Upper body is coordinated with lower limbs; do not move them individually.

9. 進步搬攔捶

（1）重心後移，左腳尖外撇，上體左轉。左掌向下畫弧，掌心向上；右掌向右前方伸展，掌心斜向下，頭隨上體轉動（圖2-48）。

(9) Step forward, Deflect, Parry and Punch

a. Shift the weight backward. Turn the upper body to the left, leading the left toes to turn outward. The left hand draws an arc downward, palm facing upward. Move the right hand to the upper right, palm facing downward diagonally. Head follows the upper body (Figure 2-48).

（2）重心前移，右腳收於左腳內側。左掌向左畫弧，再向上捲收於體前，掌心向上；同時，右掌握拳向下畫弧收於腹前，拳心向下，眼向前平視（圖2-49）。

b. Shift the weight forward. Bring the right foot in and

圖2-48　　　　　　圖2-49

place it beside the left foot. The left hand draws an arc to the left then upward and bends in front of the chest, palm facing upward. Meanwhile, turn the right hand into a fist, draw an arc to the lower left and it stops in front of the abdomen, palm facing downward. Eyes look straight ahead (Figure 2–49).

（3）右腳向前上步，腳跟著地，腳尖外撇。右拳隨之經左臂內側向前翻轉搬出，拳心向上，高與胸平，左掌順勢按至左胯旁，眼看右拳（圖2-50）。

c. The right foot steps forward with only the heel touching the ground, swinging the toes outward. The right fist punches downward with the back of the fist from the inside of the left arm at chest level, palm facing upward. The left hand falls down to the outside of the left hip. Eyes look at the right fist (Figure 2–50).

（4）重心前移，左腳跟抬起，上體右轉。右前臂內旋，右拳向右畫弧至體右側；左掌先內旋向左，再外旋向前畫弧至體前，掌心斜向下，眼看左掌（圖2-51）。

d. Shift the weight forward. Lift the left heel and turn the upper body to the right. Move the right arm inward and place the right fist at the right side of the body. Draw an arc with the left hand to the left first, then to the right and it stops in front of the body, palm facing downward diagonally. Eyes look at the left hand（Figure 2–51）.

（5）重心在右腳，左腳經右腳內側向前上一步，腳跟著地。右拳收於右腰間挎拳，拳心向上；左掌內旋坐腕，指尖斜向上，攔於體前（圖2-52）。

e. Shift the weight onto the right foot. The left foot steps forward, past the inside of the right foot, with only the heel touching the ground. The right fist draws an arc to the left then backward to the right side of the waist, palm facing up. Move the left hand forward to parry in front of the body, palm facing right, fingers pointing upward（Figure 2–52）.

圖2-50　　圖2-51　　　　　圖2-52

（6）重心前移，左腿屈膝前弓，右腿自然伸直，成左弓步。同時，右拳翻轉，拳眼向上，拳面向前打出，高與胸齊，左掌附於右前臂內側，眼看右拳（圖2-53）。

f. Shift the weight forward. Bend the left knee and extend the right leg to form a left "Bow Step". At the same time, the right fist punches forward at the chest level, the eye of the fist facing upward. The left hand is inside of the right arm. Eyes look at the right fist (Figure 2-53).

【要領】

（1）重心後坐，腰帶掌分要協調一致，重心前移，收腳收手要沉胯呼氣。

（2）上步搬拳、弓步打拳要連貫一氣，不可斷勁。

（3）重心前移，連續上步，上體保持正直，不可左右歪斜，也不可向前傾斜，保持上體水平前移，不可起伏。

Key Points

（1）Shift the weight backward in coordination with the waist, and the hand moves. When shifting the weight forward, move the hands or feet; sink the hips and breathe.

（2）Connect the movement smoothly, with no pause.

（3）When shifting the weight forward or stepping forward,

maintain the upper body upright; do not move the upper body to the left or right. When leaning forward, keep the body at the same height; do not move it up or down.

10. 如封似閉

（1）右拳微前送變掌，掌心向上；左掌經右臂下穿出，掌心向上，眼看兩手（圖2-54）。

(10) Withdraw and Push

a. Move the right fist forward slightly and turn it into an open palm to face upward. The left hand thrusts forward under the right forearm, palm facing upward. Eyes look at both hands (Figure 2-54).

圖2-53　　　　　　圖2-54

（2）上體右轉後坐，左腳尖蹺起。兩掌左右分開並屈臂內旋，收至胸前，掌心斜相對（圖2-55）。

b. Move the upper body backward; lift the left toes. Separate the two hands; bend the arms and rotate them inward; draw them back in front of the chest, palms facing each other diagonally (Figure 2-55).

（3）上體左轉正，兩掌翻轉向下按至腹前，眼看前方（圖2-56）。

c. Turn the upper body to face the front. Turn over both hands and push them down to the lower abdomen. Eyes look at the front (Figure 2-56).

（4）重心前移，左腳踏實，並屈膝前弓；右腳隨上體前移收至左腳側後方10公分處，腳尖點地，成右後丁步。同時，兩掌向前上按出，與肩同寬，掌心向前，腕高與肩平，眼看兩手（圖2-57）。

d. Shift the weight forward. Place the left foot on the ground solidly and bend the knee. The right foot follows the body to step to the back right of the left foot, 10 cm apart, only the toes touching the ground to form a right back "T Bow Step". At the same time, push both hands forward at shoulder's width. The palms are facing forward, the wrists at shoulder's level.

Eyes look at both hands (Figure 2–57).

【要領】

（1）重心後移，兩掌左右分開時要鬆胯、斂臀，斜身調臂，以腰帶動。

（2）重心前移，兩掌推按收右腳時，要沉胯呼氣，上體不可上竄。

Key Points

（1）When shifting the weight backward and separating the two hands, relax the waist; pull the buttock in; lean backward slightly to adjust the arms; movement is led by the waist.

（2）When shifting the weight forward and pushing both

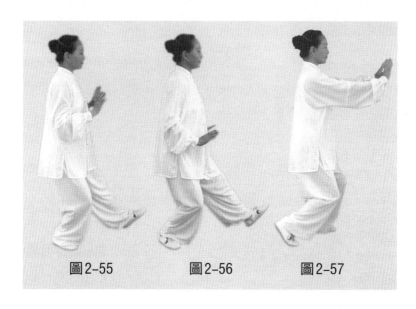

圖2-55　　　圖2-56　　　圖2-57

hands or moving the right foot, sink the hips and breathe; do not raise the upper body up.

第二組

11. 開合手

（1）以右腳掌和左腳跟為軸，上體向右依次碾轉，兩腳踏實。兩掌同時翻轉，掌心相對收至胸前，指尖向上，兩掌左右拉分，與肩同寬，眼看前方（圖 2-58）。

Group 2

(11) Opening and Closing Hands

a. When pivoting on the right forefoot and the left heel, turn the upper body to the right. Place both feet on the ground solidly. Turn both hands over and bring them in front of the chest, palms facing each other, fingers pointing upward. Separate both hands apart to shoulder's width. Eyes look at the front (Figure 2-58).

（2）重心移向左腳，右腳跟提起。同時，兩掌相合，與頭同寬，掌心相對，眼從兩掌中間向前看（圖2-59）。

b. Shift the weight to the left foot and raise the right heel. At the same time, bring the hands closer to head's width, palms facing each other. Eyes look at the front between the hands（Figure 2-59）.

【要領】

（1）開手時要吸氣，注意開胸、鬆肩。

（2）合手時要呼氣，注意鬆胯、斂臀、氣沉丹田。

Key Points

（1）When separating the hands apart, open the chest; sink the shoulders; inhale.

（2）When bringing the hands closer, sink the hips and breathe; do not push the buttock out; breathe through the abdomen.

圖2-58　　　　　　圖2-59

12. 右單鞭

（1）上體稍左轉，重心移於左腳，右腳向右橫開一步，腳跟著地，腳尖稍外撇。同時，兩掌內旋，虎口相對，掌心向外，略向左前推掌，眼看左掌（圖2-60）。

（12）Single Whip – Right

a. Turn the upper body to the left slightly and shift the weight on to the left foot. The right foot steps sideward with only the heel touching the ground, swinging the toes outward slightly. At the same time, rotate both palms inward, the tiger mouth facing each other, palms facing outward. Push both

圖2-60   圖2-61

hands to the left front slightly. Eyes are looking at the left hand (Figure 2-60).

（2）重心右移成右側弓步（橫襠步），兩掌向左右分開，平舉於身體兩側，掌心轉向外，指尖向上，眼看左手（圖2-61）。

b. Shift the weight to the right and bend the right leg to form a right side Bow Step. Separate the two hands to sides of the body at the shoulder level, palms facing outward, fingers pointing upward. Eyes look at the left hand (Figure 2-61).

【要領】

（1）成側弓步與分掌要同時完成。

（2）定勢時，上體正直舒鬆，沉肩、墜肘、塌腕，配合呼氣，氣向下沉；頭向左轉，眼看左掌。

Key Points

（1）Separate hands at the same time while making the Bow Step.

（2）When the movement settled, keep the upper body upright and comfortable; sink the shoulders, elbows, wrists and hips; breathe through the abdomen. Turn the head to the left. Eyes look at the left hand.

13. 肘底捶

（1）重心左移，上體稍左轉，右腳尖內扣。右
前臂外旋，使掌心向上，右掌同時向內掩裹畫弧至右
肩前，左掌向左向下畫弧，眼看右掌（圖2-62）。

(13) Fist under the Elbow

a. Shift the weight to the left. Turn the upper body to the
left slightly. Swing the right toes inward. Rotate the right forearm outward and turn the palm to face up in front of the right
shoulder. The left hand draws an arc to the lower left. Eyes
look at the right hand (Figure 2–62).

（2）重心右移，上體右轉，左腳收至右腳內
側。同時，右掌翻轉，手心向下，屈收至右胸前；左
前臂外旋，使掌心轉向上，經腹前向右畫弧，與右掌
上下相對，兩臂成抱球狀（圖2-63）。

b. Turn the upper body to the right and shift the weight to
the right. Bring the left foot in and place it beside the left foot.
At the same time, the right hand turns over to face downward
and bend the arm in front of the chest. Rotate the left forearm
outward and turn the hand to face up; move it past the front of
the abdomen to the right and make it correspond with the right
hand, as if holding a ball (Figure 2–63).

（3）上體左轉，左腳向左前方繞擺上步，腳跟著地，腳尖外撇。同時，左掌經右臂下向上向左畫弧，掌心向內，高與頭平；右掌經左胸前畫弧下落至右胯旁，手心向下，眼看左手（圖2-64）。

c. Turn the upper body to the left. The left foot steps to the left front with only the heel on the ground, swinging the toes outward. At the same time, the left hand draws an arc to the upper left and stops at the outside of the body at head level, palm facing inward. The right hand draws an arc downward to Pass the left side of the chest and stops beside the right hip, palm facing down. Eyes look at the left hand (Figure 2-64).

圖2-62　　　　圖2-63　　　　圖2-64

（4）上體左轉不停，重心移至左腳，右腳跟進半步，腳前掌在左腳後著地。同時，左臂內旋，掌心轉向外，向左向下畫弧至身體左側；右臂外旋，右掌向右向前畫弧至體前，高與頭齊，掌心斜向上，眼看前方（圖2-65）。

d. Continue to turn the upper body to the left and shift the weight onto the left foot. The right foot takes a half step and falls behind the left foot with only the forefoot touching the ground. At the same time, rotate the left arm inward to turn the palm facing outward and draw an arc to the lower left until it is at the left side of the body. Rotate the right arm outward and the hand draws an arc to the right front until it is in front of the body at head level, palm facing up diagonally. Eyes look at the front (Figure 2-65).

（5）重心後移至右腳，左腳向前墊步，腳跟著地，腳尖上蹺，成左虛步。同時，左掌收至左腰際成側立掌，再經右腕上向前劈出，指尖高與眉齊；右掌握拳，拳眼向上，收到左肘內側下方，眼看左手（圖2-66）。

e. Shift the weight onto the right leg. The left foot takes a half step forward, only the heel touching the ground, bending the knee to form a left Empty Step. Meanwhile, bring the left hand to the left side of the waist to form a "Side Standing Palm", and then the palm hacks forward over the right wrist, fingers pointing up at nose level. The right hand forms a fist under the left elbow, the eye of the fist facing up. Eyes look at the left hand (Figure 2-66).

【要領】

（1）兩掌畫弧擺動要以腰帶臂，鬆肩，沉胯。

（2）虛步劈掌、肘底藏捶幾個動作要協調一致，同時完成，呼氣落胯。

（3）在動作運轉過程中，上體保持正直，頭要領，氣下沉。

圖2-65　　圖2-66

Key Points

(1) The moving of the hand should be led by the waist; Relax shoulders and sink the hips.

(2) The hack in the Empty Step and hiding the fist are co-ordinated and finished at the same time. Sink the hips with exhaling.

(3) Keep the upper body upright. Draw the head up. Breathe through the abdomen.

14. 轉身推掌（二）

（1）左腳撤至右腳後10公分處，前腳掌先著地，再全腳踏實，上體慢慢左轉；右腳以腳跟為軸，腳尖裏扣，再將重心移於右腿，腿微屈。同時，右拳內旋向下穿，並變為掌向上舉，手心向上；左掌翻轉，手心向下收於右胸前，眼看右手（圖2-67）。

(14) Turn Body and Push (2)

a. Bring the left foot behind the right foot, about 10 cm apart, placing the forefoot on the ground first, then the entire foot. Turn the upper body to the left slowly. Pivot on the right heel, swinging the toes inward. Shift the weight onto the right leg, bending it slightly. Meanwhile, move the right fist downward and turn it into an open palm, then move it upward, palm facing up. Turn the left hand over and move it downward in front of the abdomen, palm facing downward. Eyes look at the right hand (Figure 2-67).

（２）上體左轉不停，左腿屈膝下蹲，右腳向左前邁進一步，腳跟著地。同時，右臂屈肘，右掌收至右耳旁，掌心斜向前下方，左掌向下向左畫弧，眼看前方（圖2-68）。

b. Turn the upper body to the left. Bend the left knee in a half squat. The right foot steps to the left front with only the heel touching the ground. Meanwhile, bend the right elbow, bringing the hand beside the right ear, palm facing lower front diagonally. The left hand draws an arc to the lower left. Eyes

圖2-67　　　　　圖2-68

look at the front (Figure 2-68).

（3）重心前移，左腿屈膝前弓，左腳向前踏
實；右腳隨重心前移跟步至左腳內側後方，前腳掌著
地。同時，右掌順勢向前推出，掌心向前，指尖與鼻
尖相對，左掌經左膝上摟過按於左胯旁，眼看右掌
（圖2-69）。

c. Shift the weight forward. Bend the left knee and take a step forward. The right foot follows the body and steps to the left back of the right foot, placing only the forefoot on the ground. Meanwhile, push the right hand forward at nose level, palm facing forward. Move the left hand over the left knee to the outside of the left hip. Eyes look at the right hand (Figure 2-69).

（4）重心後移於右腳，上體右轉，以左腳跟為
軸，左腳尖裏扣再踩實，並稍屈膝下沉。同時，左臂外
旋向左前方上舉，掌心向上，高與頭平；右掌隨右臂屈
肘下落至左胸前，掌心向下，眼看左手（圖2-70）。

d. Turn the upper body to the right and shift the weight onto the right leg. Pivot on the left heel, swinging the toes inward, then place the entire foot on the ground firmly. Bend the knee slightly and lower the weight. Meanwhile, rotate the left arm outward and raise it to the left front, palm facing upward at head level. Bend the forearm and the hand falls in front of the chest vertically, palm facing the downward. Eyes look at the left hand (Figure 2-70).

（5）重心下沉，右腳向右前方邁出一步，腳跟著地。同時，左臂屈肘，將左掌收於左耳旁，掌心斜向前下，右掌下按落於腹前，眼看前方（圖2-71）。

e. Lower the weight. The right foot steps to the right front with only the heel touching the ground. Meanwhile, bend the left elbow and bring the hand beside the left ear, palm facing lower front diagonally. The right hand falls in front of the abdomen. Eyes look at the front (Figure 2-71).

圖2-69　　圖2-70　　　　圖2-71

（6）上體右轉，重心前移，右腿屈膝前弓，右腳向正前踏實，左腳重心前移跟步至右腳內側成左丁步。同時，左掌順勢向前推出，掌心向前，指尖與鼻尖相對；右掌經右膝上摟過，按於右胯旁，眼看左手（圖2-72）。

f. Shift the weight forward. Turn the upper body to the right. Bend the right knee and step forward. The left foot follows the body and steps to the left side of the right foot to form a left T–Step. Meanwhile, push the left hand forward at nose level, palm facing forward. Move the right hand over the right knee to the outside of the right hip. Eyes look at the left hand (Figure 2–72).

【要領】

（1）轉身時要分清虛實轉換，重心先後移，再扣腳；推掌時要隨重心前移，用腰勁順勢前推。

（2）上步時要斜出正踩，即向斜前方上步，向正前方踏實。

（3）身法前進，推掌與摟踩要協調一致，同時動作，同時完成。

Key Points

（1）When turning the body, shift the weight backward first, then swing the toes inward. When pushing, shift the weight forward and be led by the waist.

（2）When stepping forward, toes point outward first, swing it to the front and then place the entire foot on the ground firmly.

（3）Step forward in coordination with the motions of the hands, and finish them simultaneously.

15. 玉女穿梭（二）

（1）上體右轉，左腳向左撤半步。左臂外旋，左掌向右畫弧至右胸前，掌心轉向上；右掌上提經左前臂上方向前伸探至體前，掌心斜向下，腕高與肩平，眼看右掌（圖2-73）。

（15）Fair Lady Works at Shuttles（2）

a. Turn the upper body to the right. The left foot takes a half

圖2-72　　　　圖2-73

step to the left. Rotate the left arm outward. The left hand draws an arc to the right until it is in the right front of the chest. Turn the left palm to face up. Lift the right hand over the left forearm forward in front of the body, palm facing down diagonally, and wrist at shoulder level. Eyes look at the right hand (Figure 2-73).

（2）上體左轉，重心移至左腿，右腳收至左腳內側，腳尖點地。兩掌同時自前向下向右捋，左掌捋至左胯旁，右掌捋至腹前，眼隨兩手（圖2-74）。

b. Turn the upper body to the left and shift the weight onto the left leg. Bring the right foot in and place it beside the left foot with only the toes on the ground. Pull both hands to the lower right; the left hand stops beside the left hip; the right hand stops in front of the abdomen. Eyes follow both hands (Figure 2-74).

（3）上體先稍左轉再右轉，右腳向右前方上步，腳跟著地。右前臂外旋，左前臂內旋，兩掌合舉於胸前，右掌心向內，指尖向左；左掌心向外，掌指附於右腕內側，眼看右手（圖2-75）。

c. Turn the upper body first to the left slightly, then to the right. The right foot takes a step to the right front with only the heel on the ground. Rotate the right forearm outward, the left forearm inward. Both hands meet in front of the chest, the right palm facing in, fingers pointing left; the left palm facing outward, fingers touching the inside of the right wrist. Eyes look at the right hand (Figure 2–75).

（4）上體右轉不停，重心前移，右腿屈膝前弓，左腳隨上體前移跟步至右腳內側後方，腳前掌著地。右掌自左向前畫平弧，掌心轉向上，左掌隨右掌轉動，眼看右掌（圖2-76）。

d. Continue to turn the upper body to the right and shift the weight forward. Bend the right knee forward. The left foot follows the body to step backward to the left back of the right

圖2-74　　　　圖2-75　　　　圖2-76

foot, forefoot on the ground. Move the right hand from the left side to the front, palm facing upward. The left hand follows the right hand. Eyes look at the right hand (Figure 2-76).

（5）重心後移，左腳踏實，上體左轉，右腳再向右前方上一步，腳跟著地。右臂屈肘內旋向右向後畫平弧，而後右掌翹腕至右肩前上方，掌心斜向上，左掌隨之畫弧後收至左腰際，眼看前方（圖2-77）。

e. Shift the weight backward. Place the left foot on the ground firmly. Turn the upper body to the left. The right foot takes a step to the right front with only the heel on the ground. the right arm rotates inward, and draws an arc to the right back then stop in front of the right shoulder, palm facing up diagonally. The left hand falls to the left side of the waist. Eyes look at the front (Figure 2-77).

（6）重心前移，右腿屈膝前弓，左腿自然伸直成右弓步，上體右轉。右掌上架於右額前上方，掌心斜向上；左掌前按至體前，掌心向前，指尖向上，與鼻尖相對，眼看左手（圖2-78）。

f. Shift the weight forward. Bend the right knee forward and extend the left leg to form a right Bow Step. Continue to turn the upper body to the right. Raise the right hand over the right side of the forehead, palm facing upward diagonally. Push the left hand in front of the body, palm facing forward, fingers pointing up at node level. Eyes look at the left hand (Figure 2-78).

（7）重心後移，右腳尖抬起略內扣，上體左轉。右前臂外旋，右掌翻轉下落於體前，手心向上，右腕高與肩平；左掌向右畫弧後收至右肘內側，手心向下，眼看右掌（圖2-79）。

g. Shift the weight backward. List the right toes and swing them inward. Turn the upper body to the left. Rotate the right forearm outward, palm facing up, and wrist at shoulder level.

圖2-77　　　　圖2-78　　　　圖2-79

The left palm draws an arc to the right and stops at the inside of the right elbow, palm facing down. Eyes look at the right hand (Figure 2–79).

（8）重心前移，使右腳踏實，上體左轉不停。左掌從右前臂上穿出，並自右向左畫弧抹掌，右掌收於左肘內側下方，兩掌心上下斜相對，眼看左手（圖2-80）。

h. Shift the weight forward. Place the right foot on the ground firmly. Continue to turn the upper body to the left. Thrust the left hand out from the beneath of the right forearm and move it from the right to the left. Bring the right hand in and place it at the lower inside of the left elbow. Both palms face in. Eyes look at the left hand (Figure 2–80).

（9）上體右轉，左腳收至右腳內側。兩掌自前同時向下向後将，右掌将至右胯旁，左掌将至腹前，眼隨兩手（圖2-81）。

i. Turn the upper body to the right. Bring the left foot in and place it beside the right foot. Pull both hands to the lower back; the right hand stops beside the left hip; the left hand stops in front of the abdomen. Eyes follow both hands (Figure 2–81).

（10）左腳向左前方上步，腳跟著地。左前臂外旋，右前臂內旋，兩掌上舉合於胸前，左掌心向裏，掌指向右；右掌心向外，掌指附於左腕內側，眼看左掌（圖2-82）。

j. The left foot takes a step to the left front with only the heel on the ground. Rotate the left forearm outward, the right forearm inward. Both hands meet in front of the chest, the left palm facing in, fingers pointing the left; the right palm facing outward, fingers touching the inside of the left wrist. Eyes look at the left hand (Figure 2-82).

（11）重心前移，上體左轉，右腳隨之跟進至左

圖2-80　　　　　圖2-81　　　圖2-82

腳內後側，腳前掌著地。左掌自右向前畫平弧，掌心轉向上，右掌隨之轉動，眼看左手（圖2-83）。

k. Turn the upper body to the left and shift the weight forward. The right foot follows the body to step backward to the right back of the left foot, forefoot on the ground. Move the left hand from the right side to the front, palm facing upward. The right hand follows the right hand. Eyes look at the left hand (Figure 2–83).

（12）重心後移，上體右轉，左腳再向左前方上一步。左臂屈肘內旋向左向後畫平弧，而後左掌翹腕至左肩前上方，掌心斜向上，右掌隨之畫弧下落後收於右腰際，眼看前方（圖2-84）。

l. Shift the weight backward. Turn the upper body to the right. The left foot takes a step to the left front. Bend the left arm and rotate it inward, it drawing an arc to the left back and stopping in front of the left shoulder, palm facing up diagonally. The right hand falls to the right side of the waist. Eyes look at the front (Figure 2–84).

（13）上體左轉，重心前移，左腿屈膝前弓，右腿自然伸直，成左弓步。左掌上架於左額前上方，掌心斜向上，右掌掌心向前按出至體前，指尖與鼻尖相對，眼看右掌（圖2-85）。

m. Shift the weight forward. Turn the upper body to the left. Bend the left knee forward and extend the right leg to form a left Bow Step. Raise the left hand over the left side of the forehead, palm facing upward diagonally. Push the right hand in front of the body, palm facing forward, fingers pointing up at node level. Eyes look at the right hand（Figure 2–85）.

【要領】

（1）上步平擺掌、跟步內旋臂、弓步架推掌要力求平穩、連貫、圓活，協調一致。

（2）上步要順遂，不宜開胯過大，上體歪扭。

圖2-83　　　圖2-84　　　　圖2-85

（3）弓步時，兩腳不要踩在一條線上，推掌、架掌要與弓步方向一致。

（4）定勢架掌臂要撐圓，不可聳肩，抬肘或彎臂弧度不可過大，架手不可過低。

（5）上體要保持正直，鬆胯，沉氣。

Key Points

（1）Keep the motions steady, connected smoothly and co-ordinated with each other.

（2）When stepping forward, do not make a big step; do not bow forward.

（3）When making the Bow Step (Gong Bu), do not stand on the same line with both feet. Push hands in the same direction as the Bow Step and parrying.

（4）When the movement is completed, the arm is arched; do not raise the shoulder; do not bend the arm or elbow too much. The parrying hand is no lower than the forehead.

（5）Keep the upper body upright. Sink the hips. Breathe through the abdomen.

16. 右左蹬腳（二）

（1）重心後移，左腳尖內扣，上體右轉。左臂外旋，左掌翻轉落於體前，掌心向上，腕高與肩平；右掌向左畫弧後收至左肘內側，掌心向下，眼看左手

（圖2-86）。

(16) Kick with the Heel—Right and Left(2)

a. Shift the weight backward and swing the left toes inward. Turn the upper body to the right. Rotate the left arm outward. Turn the left hand over in front of the body, palm facing up and wrist at shoulder level. The right hand draws an arc to the left and stops inside of the left elbow, palm facing down. Eyes look at the left hand (Figure 2-86).

（2）重心前移，上體左轉。右掌從左前臂上方穿出，向上向右畫弧展開，左掌向下向左畫弧至右腰側，頭隨上體轉動（圖2-87）。

圖2-86　　　　　　圖2-87

b. Shift the weight forward. Turn the upper body to the left. Move the right hand over the left forearm then to the right front. The left hand draws an arc to the lower left and stops at the right side of the waist. Head follows the upper body (Figure 2–87).

（3）上體右轉，右腳收於左腳內側。右掌向下向左向上畫弧，左掌向左向上向右畫弧至胸前，兩腕交疊，兩掌交叉合抱，右掌在外，掌心均向內，眼看右前方（圖2-88）。

c. Turn the upper body to the right. Place the right foot beside the left foot. Move both hands upward to the chest to form "X". The left hand is on the inside, the right one outside. Both palms face the body. Then Eyes look at the right front (Figure 2–88).

（4）左腿微屈站穩，右腿屈膝提起，右腳向左前方（約30°）慢慢蹬出，腳尖上勾，腳跟高過腰部。兩掌分別向右前方和左方畫弧分開，掌心向外，腕與肩平，兩臂伸展，肘微屈，右臂與右腿上下相對，眼看右手（圖2-89）。

d. Bend the left knee slightly and stand on it firmly. Lift the right leg, bending the knee and kicking to the left front (about 30°) slowly with the heel at waist level, toes pointing backward. At the same time, move the two hands to the sides of the body, palms facing outward, elbows bending at shoulder level. The right elbow is above the right leg. Eyes look at the right hand (Figure 2–89).

（5）右腿屈收，重心下降，右腳向右前方落下，腳跟著地。右前臂外旋，使掌心向上，稍向內收；左掌下落，經腰間向前向上畫弧伸至右肘內側，掌心向下，眼看右掌（圖2-90）。

e. Bring the right leg in. Lower the weight. The right foot steps forward with only the heel on the ground. Rotate the right arm outward to turn the palm facing up, and bring it in slight-

圖2-88　　　圖2-89　　　圖2-90

ly. The left hand falls and draws an arc past the waist to the upper front until it is at the inside of the right elbow, palm facing
down. Eyes look at the right hand (Figure 2-90).

（6）重心前移，右腳踏實，上體右轉。左掌從
右前臂上方穿出向上向左畫弧展開，掌心向下，右掌
向下向右畫弧至腰側，頭隨上體轉動（圖2-91）。

f. Shift the weight forward. Place the right foot on the
ground firmly. Turn the upper body to the right. Move the left
hand over the right forearm then to the left front. The right
hand draws an arc to the lower right and stops at the left side
of the waist. Head follows the upper body (Figure 2-91).

（7）上體左轉，左腳收於右腳內側。左掌向下
向右向上畫弧，右掌向右向上向左畫弧至胸前，兩腕
交疊，兩掌交叉合抱，左掌在外，掌心均向裏，眼看
左前方（圖2-92）。

g. Turn the upper body to the left. Place the left foot beside the right foot. Move both hands up to the chest to form
"X". The right hand is on the inside, the left one outside. Both
palms face the body. Eyes look at the right front (Figure 2-92).

（8）右腿微屈站穩，左腿屈膝提起，左腳向左

前方約30°方向蹬出，腳尖上勾，腳跟不低於腰部。兩掌分別向左前方和右方畫弧分開，掌心向外，腕與肩平，兩臂伸展，肘微屈，左臂與左腿上下相對，眼看左手（圖2-93）。

h. Bend the right knee slightly and stand on it firmly. Lift the left leg, bending the knee and kicking to the left front (about 30°) slowly with the heel at waist level, toes pointing backward. At the same time, move both hands to the sides of the body, palms facing outward, elbows bending at shoulder level. The left elbow is above the left leg. Eyes look at the left hand (Figure 2–93).

圖2-91　　　　圖2-92　　　　圖2-93

【要領】

（1）完成動作要柔和連貫，手腳配合要協調一致，蹬腳、分掌要同時完成。

（2）獨立支撐時重心要平穩，支撐腿要微屈，要頂頭，立腰，沉肩，展臂，自然呼吸。

（3）蹬腳時，不可彎腰、低頭，腿膝部要展直，不可彎曲，兩臂外撐。腳尖上勾，腿跟用力。

Key Points

（1）Complete the entire movement smoothly. Hands are coordinated with the feet. The separating of the hands and the kick are synchronized and finish at the same time.

（2）When standing on one leg, maintain the weight steady. Bend the supporting leg slightly; draw the upper body up; sink the shoulders; extend the arms; keep the waist upright; breathe naturally.

（3）When Kicking, do not bend forward or lean backward; extend the leg. The elbow should not be rigid; palms are arched outward; toes point upward; deliver the energy to the heel.

17. 掩手肱捶

（1）左小腿屈收，右腿屈蹲，左腳收落於右腳內側。兩臂外旋，兩肘墜合，兩手掩合於頭前，與頭同寬，掌心向內，眼看兩手（圖2-94）。

(17) Hide and Roll Arm Punch

　　a. Bend the left lower leg and bring it in. Bend the right leg in a half squat. Place the left foot beside the right foot. Rotate both arms outward. Sink both elbows inward. Move both hands together in front of the face, apart at the head's width, palms facing in. Eyes look at the both hand (Figure 2-94).

　　（2）左腳尖上蹺，重心下落，左腳跟擦地向左偏前開步，上體稍右轉。兩臂內旋，兩掌翻轉下落，上下交叉相疊於小腹右側，左掌壓於右掌背上，掌心均向下，眼看兩手（圖2-95）。

圖2-94　　　　　　　　　　圖2-95

b. Raise the left toes. Lower the weight. The left heel wipes to the left front. Turn the upper body to the right slightly. Rotate both arms inward. Turn both hands over and move them to the right side of the abdomen. The left palm is on the back of the right hand, both palms facing down. Eyes look at the both hand (Figure 2-95).

（3）上體左轉正，重心左移於兩腿之間。兩掌向兩側開分，高與肩平，前臂內旋，掌心轉向外，眼看前方（圖2-96）。

c. Turn the upper body to the left to face forward. Shift the weight between the legs. Separate both hands at shoulder level and rotate them inward to turn the palms outward. Eyes look at the front (Figure 2-96).

（4）右移重心，上體微右轉。兩臂外旋，兩肘內合，左掌擺至體前，掌心向上，高與肩平；右掌變拳，屈臂合於胸前，拳心向上，眼看左手（圖2-97）。

d. Shift the weight to the right slightly. Turn the upper body to the right. Rotate both arms outward. Sink both elbows inward. Move the left hand in front of the body at the shoulder level, palms facing up. Turn the right hand into a fist and bend the arm in front of the chest, palms facing up. Eyes look at the left hand (Figure 2-97).

（5）重心左移，上體左轉，轉腰順肩，成左弓步。右拳旋轉向前方衝打，拳心轉向下；左掌後收，掌心貼於左腹部，指尖向右，眼看右拳（圖2-98）。

e. Shift the weight to the left. Turn the upper body to the left to face forward and form a left Bow Step. The right fist punches forward and turns over to face downward. Bring the left hand in and place the palm at the left side of the abdomen, fingers pointing right. Eyes look at the right hand (Figure 2-98).

圖2-96　　　　　圖2-97

【要領】

（1）兩腿屈蹲時，上體右轉，重心右移，兩臂外旋，兩肘內合。屈膝縮胯，含胸拔背，吸氣蓄勁。

（2）衝拳發勁與蹬腿轉腰協調一致，以腰催臂，把力發到拳面，用周身爆發力衝拳。同時，頂頭順肩，豎脊轉腰，實腹呼氣，兩臂前衝後拉，以呼氣助力。

（3）衝拳後，右臂要自然放鬆，鬆握拳。

（4）左腳出腳方向為左前30°～40°，衝拳方向與弓步夾角約60°，即正前偏右。

Key Points

（1）When bending both legs, turn the upper body to the right and shift the weight to the right. Rotate both arms out-

圖2-98　　　　　　圖2-99

ward; Sink the elbows inward; bend the knees and pull the hips in; draw the back up and pull the check in; inhale to increase the energy.

(2) Punch and kick are coordinated and finished at the same time. Waist leads the arm; the shoulder follows. Deliver the force to the fist with burst force. Draw the head up. Exhale through the abdomen to increase the force. Push the two arms in opposite directions.

(3) After punching, relax the arms; loose the fist.

(4) The left foot steps $30° \sim 40°$ to the left front. The direction of the punching is $60°$ from the left foot.

18. 野馬分鬃（二）

（1）上體左轉，右拳變掌向下畫弧至腹前，掌心向下；左掌以拇指為軸，四指順時針向下轉動（圖2-99）。

(18) Splitting Wild Horse's Mane(2)

a. Turn the upper body to the left. The right hand changes the fist into an open palm and draws an arc down to the abdomen, palm facing down. Pivoting on the left thumb, the left hand turns downward clockwise (Figure 2–99).

（2）重心右移，上體右轉。右臂內旋，右掌翻轉向外，並向上向右畫弧，屈臂置於右肩前，拇指向下，四指尖向左；左臂外旋，掌心轉向內，掌指背貼於右前臂內側，隨之畫弧，兩臂撐圓，眼看右手（圖2-100）。

b. Shift the weight to the right. Turn the upper body to the right. Rotate the right arm inward and turn the palm facing outward. Move the right hand in an arc to the upper right and bend the arm in front of the right shoulder, the thumb pointing down, fingers pointing left. Rotate the left arm outward and turn the palm facing inward, fingers at the inside of the right forearm. The left hand follows right arm to draw an arc. Both arms are arched. Eyes look at the right hand (Figure 2-100).

（3）重心左移，上體左轉。右臂外旋，左臂內旋，兩掌成橫掌，掌心向左前方，指尖向外，橫於腹前，腰腹彈性發力，眼看兩手（圖2-101）。

c. Shift the weight to the left. Turn the upper body to the left. Rotate the right arm outward. Rotate the left arm inward. Both hands are facing the left, fingers pointing out. The force from the waist and abdomen leads both hands pushing to the left in front of the abdomen. Eyes look at the both hand (Figure 2-101).

（4）重心右移，腰向右回轉，兩掌自右向左畫弧，成俯掌於腹前，指尖皆向前，眼看右掌（圖2-102）。

d. Shift the weight to the right. Turn the waist to the right. Move both hands from the right to the left in front of the abdomen, fingers pointing for ward. Eyes look at the right hand (Figure 2-102).

（5）重心後移，左腿屈膝提起。左臂外旋，左掌向左向下向右再向前上畫弧翻轉，掌心向上，托於左膝上方；右掌向下向右上畫弧橫於身體右側，掌心向外，眼看前方（圖2-103）。

e. Shift the weight backward. Lift the left knee. Rotate the

圖2-100　　　　　圖2-101

left arm inward. Move the left hand to the left, then downward, then to the right, then forward and turn it over to face up over the left knee. Move right hand downward then to the right and stop it at the right side of the body, palm facing outward, fingers pointing forward. Eyes look at the front (Figure 2–103).

（6）左腳向前上步，重心前移，成左弓步。左掌向前穿出，掌心向上，指尖向前，左腕高與頭平；右掌撐至身體右方，掌心向外，指尖斜向上，腕高與肩平，眼看左掌（圖2-104）。

f. The left foot steps forward. Shift the weight forward and form a left Bow Step. The left hand goes forward to the head

圖2-102　　　　　　　圖2-103

level, palm facing up, fingers pointing forward; the right hand goes to the right side of the body, bending the elbow slightly, palm facing outward, fingers pointing up, wrist at shoulder level. Eyes look at the left hand (Figure 2–104).

（7）重心後移，左腳尖外撇，上體左轉。左臂內旋，左掌心翻轉向外，並稍屈臂外撐；右臂亦外旋，右掌稍下落內收，眼看左掌（圖2-105）。

g. Shift the weight backward. Swing the left toes outward. Turn the upper body to the left. Rotate the left arm inward and bend it outward, turning the hand to face outward. Rotate the right arm outward and bring the hand in. Eyes look at the left

圖2-104　　　　圖2-105

hand（Figure 2–105）.

（8）重心前移，上體左轉，右腿屈膝向前提收。右掌向下畫弧，經體側前舉，托於右膝上方，掌心向上；左掌左擺橫於體左側，掌心向外，指尖斜向上，眼看右手（圖2–106）。

h. Shift the weight backward. Turn the waist to the left. Lift the right knee. Move the right hand downward then raise it forward from the outside of the body to the upside of the right knee. Move the left hand to the left side of the body, palm facing outward, fingers pointing up. Eyes look at the right hand（Figure 2–106）.

（9）右腳向前上步，重心前移，成右弓步。右掌向前穿靠，掌心向上，指尖向前，腕高與頭平；左掌撐至身體左側，掌心向外，指尖斜向上，腕高與肩平，眼看右手（圖2–107）。

i. The right foot steps forward. Shift the weight forward and form a right Bow Step. The right hand goes forward to the head level, palm facing up, fingers pointing forward; the left hand goes to the left side of the body, bending the elbow slightly, palm facing outward, fingers pointing up, wrist at shoulder level. Eyes look at the right hand（Figure 2–107）.

【要領】

（1）此勢選自陳式太極拳，因此要在轉換時做到轉腰旋臂，轉膝旋踝，以身帶手，表現出纏繞折疊的特點。

（2）在捌掌折疊時，轉腰帶臂，短促發力，動作要頓挫分明，斷而復連，張弛剛柔，變化有序，富有彈性。

（3）穿靠時，要腳跟先著地而穿掌，力點在上臂與肩關節上。

Key Points

（1）Maintain the upper body upright; do not bend the upper body forward or backward; keep the chest relaxed and comfort-

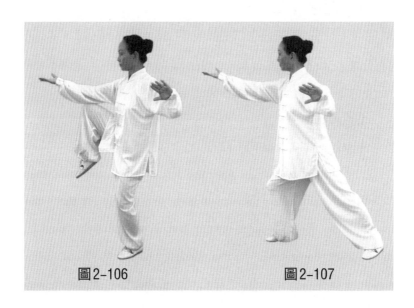

圖2-106　　　　　圖2-107

able. Move arms in arc. The upper body follows the waist to turn around.

(2) For the Bow Step, feet should rest on both sides of the center of the body and stand on two parallel lines separately, which is no more 30 cm apart. The feet and hands are moving at the same and even speed.

(3) When separating the hands, the upper hand acts pushing outward; the lower hand acts pushing downward. Move feet gently and fast. Always lift the heel or forefoot first, and place the forefoot or heel to the ground first. Do not make a heavy step.

第三組

19. 雲手（三）

（1）重心左移，右腳尖內扣，上體左轉。右前臂內旋，右掌翹腕右旋，向左擺至右肩前；左掌微向左撐，掌心向左，眼看右掌（圖2-108）。

Group 3
(19) Cloud Hands(3)

a. Shifting the weight onto the left, leading the right toes to swing inward, turn the upper body to the left. At the same time, rotate the right arm inward and move the right hand to draw an arc downward, then to the left, cross it the front of the abdomen and stop it in front of the right shoulder. Move the left hand towards left, palm facing left. Eyes look at the right hand (Figure 2–108).

（2）重心右移，上體右轉，左腳跟隨之碾動。右掌翻轉向外，橫掌右擺至身體右側；左掌自左向下經腹前向右畫弧，掌心隨之翻轉向上，眼看右手（圖2–109）。

b. Turn the upper body to the right, shifting the weight to the right, leading the left forefoot off the ground. At the same time, the right hand draws an arc upward to the right side of the body. The left hand draws an arc to the left front, downward, and then stops in the front of the abdomen, turning the

圖2–108   圖2–109

palm to face up. Eyes look at the right hand (Figure 2-109).

（3）重心左移，上體左轉。左掌掌心向內，自右向上經面前向左畫弧雲轉，指尖與眉同高；右掌向下經腹前向左畫弧雲轉，掌心由外轉向內，眼隨左手（圖2-110）。

c. Shifting the weight to the left, turn the upper body to the left. The left hand draws an arc from the right, passing in front of the face, towards the left, fingers at eyebrow level, palm facing inward. The right hand draws an arc downward past the abdomen towards the left, turning the palm to face inward. Eyes look at the left hand (Figure 2-110).

（4）上體左轉不停，右腳收於左腳內側落地，兩腳平行向前，相距10～20公分。兩掌雲至身體左側逐漸翻轉，左掌心轉向外，右掌雲至左肘內側，掌心轉向內，眼看右手（圖2-111）。

d. Continue to turn the upper body to the left. The right foot takes a small step towards the left foot to make the feet parallel with each other, toes pointing the front. The feet are 20～30 cm apart. Eyes look at the right hand (Figure 2-111).

（5）重心右移，上體右轉，右掌自左經面前向右畫弧雲轉，指尖高與眉齊，左掌向下經腹前向右畫弧雲轉，眼看右手（圖2-112）。

e. Shifting the weight to the right, turn the upper body to the right. The right hand draws an arc from the left, passing in front of the face, towards the right, fingers at eyebrow level. The left hand draws an arc downward past the abdomen towards the right, turning the palm to face inward. Eyes look at the right hand (Figure 2-112).

（6）上體繼續右轉，左腳向左側開步，腳尖仍向前。兩掌雲至身體右側，逐漸翻轉，右掌心轉向外，左掌雲至右肘內側，掌心轉向內，眼看右手（圖2-113）。

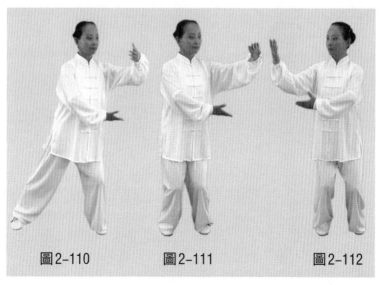

圖2-110　　　圖2-111　　　圖2-112

f. Continue to turn the upper body to the right. The left foot takes a small step towards the left side, toes pointing the front. Both hands are at the right side of the body and turn over them gradually, the right hand facing outward. The left hand is at the inside of the right elbow, palm facing inward. Eyes look at the right hand (Figure 2–113).

（7）重心左移，上體左轉，左掌經面前向左畫弧雲轉，右掌向下經腹前畫弧向左雲轉，眼看左手（圖2-114）。

g. Shifting the weight to the left, turn the upper body to the left. The left hand draws an arc passing in front of the face

圖2-113　　　　圖2-114

towards the left, fingers at eyebrow. The right hand draws an arc downward past the abdomen towards the left. Eyes look at the left hand（Figure 2–114）.

（8）上體左轉不停，右腳收於左腳內側落地，兩腳平行向前，相距10～20公分。兩掌雲至身體左側逐漸翻轉，左掌心轉向外，右掌雲至左肘內側，掌心轉向內，眼看左手（圖2–115）。

h. Continue to turn the upper body to the left. The right foot takes a small step towards the left foot to make both feet parallel with each other, toes pointing the front. The feet are 20～30 cm apart. Both hands are at the left side of the body

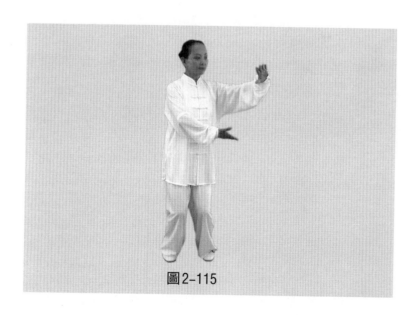

圖2-115

and turn over them gradually, the left hand facing outward. The right hand is at the inside of the left elbow, palm facing inward. Eyes look at the left hand (Figure 2–115).

（9）上述（5）（6）（7）（8）動作重複一次，但最後收併右腳時腳尖內扣約45°落地（圖2–116、圖2–117、圖2–118、圖2–119）。

i. Repeat (5), (6), (7), (8). Finish them with the right toes pointing 45° inward (Figure 2–116 ～ Figure 2–119).

【要領】
（1）雲手轉腰與側行步要協調配合，兩手連續交

圖2–116   圖2–117

叉畫立圓，動作中要以腰為軸帶動上肢，眼隨上手。

（2）側行步時重心要平穩，移動腿為虛，支撐腿為實，兩腿要虛實分明；上體保持正直，不要左右搖晃，或彎腰凸臀，或上下起伏。

（3）雲手及側行步要保持速度均勻。

Key Points

（1）The body, feet and hands are co-ordinated. Maintain curved and rounded arms with energy. Waist is acting as an axel when the upper body rotates. The motions of the hands are led by the waist. Eyes follow the upper hand.

（2）While stepping sideward, lift or place the foot lightly. The supporting leg is solid. There should not be any heavy

圖2-118　　　　圖2-119

steps. The upper body should not swing or make any unnecessary movements up and down. Do not bow the head. Do not bend the waist. Always maintain an upright upper body.

(3) Keep an even speed for moving hands and feet.

20. 獨立打虎

（1）重心右移，左腳向身後撤一步，右腿屈膝前弓。左掌掌心翻轉向上向下畫弧收於腹前，右掌掌心翻轉向下，經左前臂上方穿出，向前伸探至體前，腕高與肩平，眼看右手（圖2-120）。

(20) Stand on One Leg and Hit a Tiger

a. Shift the weight to the right. The left foot takes a step backward. Bend the right knee forward. Turn the left hand over to face up and draw an arc down to the abdomen. Turn the right hand over to face downward, thrust forward above the left forearm in front of the body, wrist at eye level. Eyes look at the right hand (Figure 2-120).

（2）重心移至左腿，上體左轉，右腳尖內扣。兩掌向下經腹前向左畫弧，視線隨上體轉向左後方（圖2-121）。

b. Shift weight onto the left leg. Turn the upper body to the left, swinging the toes inward. Both hands draw arcs downward across the abdomen to the left. Eyes follow the upper body to the left back (Figure 2-121).

（3）兩掌逐漸握拳，左拳經體側屈臂上舉至左額前上方，拳心向外，拳眼斜向下；右拳屈臂收於左胸前，拳心向裏，拳眼向上。左腿微屈站穩，右腿屈膝提起，右腳收至襠前，腳尖上蹺並內扣，頭轉向右前方，眼看前方（圖2-122）。

c. Turn both hands into fists gradually. Raise the left fist from the outside of the body and bend the arm in front of the left forehead, palm facing outward, the eye of the fist facing downward diagonally. Bend the right arm in the left front of the

圖2-120　　圖2-121　　圖2-122

chest, palm facing inward, the eye of the fist facing up. Bend the left leg and stand on it firmly. Lift the right knee, foot in between the legs, toes pointing up and inward. Head faces the right front. Eyes look at the front (Figure 2–122).

【要領】

（1）兩掌向左畫弧時，頭要左轉，眼向左後方看；提右腿貫拳時，頭轉向正前方，眼看前方。

（2）左腿獨立支撐時，胯部要放鬆；右腿提膝時，右腳尖要上蹺內扣，腳跟裏勾。

Key Points

（1）When both hands move to the left, turn the head to the left; eyes look at the left back. When raising the right knee and fists, turn the head to face the front; eyes look at the front.

（2）When standing on the left leg, relax the hip. When raising the right knee, the foot is arched.

21. 右分腳

（1）上體微右轉，右腳內收，腳尖下垂。兩拳變掌疊抱於胸前，右掌在外，掌心皆向裏，眼看右前方（圖2-123）。

(21) Separate Feet – Right

a. Turn the upper body to the right slightly. Bring the right foot in, toes pointing downward. Turn both hands into open palms and form an "X" in front of the chest. The right palm is on the outside, both palms facing the body. Eyes look at the front (Figure 2-123).

（2）右腳面展平，腳尖向右前上方慢慢踢出，高過腰部。兩掌同時向右前方和左方畫弧分開，掌心均向外，指尖向上，腕高與肩平，兩臂撐舉，肘關節微屈，右臂與右腿上下相對，眼看右手（圖2-124）。

b. Stretch the right foot, kick to the right front with the toes, at waist level. Then separate both hands, the right one goes to the right front, the left one goes to the left, both palms

圖2-123　　　　　　圖2-124

facing outward, fingers pointing up, wrist at shoulder level. Arms are arched; elbows are bent. The right arm is above the right leg. Eyes look at the right hand (Figure 2–124).

【要領】

（1）右腳下垂時，右大腿保持穩定，上體保持正直。

（2）分腳時兩手要外撐，與分手要協調配合；上體穩定，不可低頭、彎腰、屈腿、揚臂；自然呼吸。

Key Points

（1）When the right toes pointing downward, maintain the leg steady; do not bend the upper body forward or backward.

（2）When kicking, push the hands outward and coordinate with each other; maintain the upper body steady; do not bow the head or bend the waist; do not bend the leg or raise the arm; Breathe naturally.

22. 雙峰貫耳

（1）右腿屈膝，小腿回收，腳尖下垂。兩臂屈肘外旋，在胸前相合，兩掌經面前畫弧平行下落於右膝上方，掌心翻轉向上，眼看前方（見圖2-125）。

(22) Strike Ears with Both Fists

a. Bend the right knee and bring back the lower leg, toes pointing downward. Rotate both elbows outward and stop them in front of the chest. Then move both hands downward to the sides of the right thigh, hands facing upward. Eyes look at the front（Figure 2-125）.

（2）兩掌握拳經右大腿兩側分別落於腰兩側，拳心向上。同時，左腿屈膝落胯，右腳向前落步，腳跟著地，眼看前方（圖2-126）。

b. Form fists with both hands and pull them up beside the hips, palm facing up. At the same time, the right foot steps forward with only the heel touching the ground. Eyes watch the front（Figure 2-126）.

圖2-125　　　　圖2-126

（3）重心前移成右弓步，兩拳同時經兩側向前上方畫弧貫打，高與耳齊，與頭同寬，拳眼斜向下，兩臂半屈成鉗形，眼看前方（圖2-127）。

c. The right foot steps to the right front and shift the weight forward to form a right "Bow Step". Form fists with both hands gradually and punch from either side of the body in front of the face to form a " \ / " shape at ear level. Both fists are coordinated with each other and the eyes of them face downward diagonally; fists are about 20 cm apart. Eyes look ahead (Figure 2-127).

【要領】

（1）右腳向前落步時左腿屈膝下蹲，同時鬆胯，斂臀。

（2）弓步和貫拳方向與右分腳相同，均為偏右30°，同時要注意頂頭，直腰，沉肩，墜肘，上體不可前傾，低頭。

Key Points

(1) When the right foot stepping forward, bend the left knee in a half squat; relax the hips; pull the buttocks in.

(2) The direction of the Bow Step and the punching is the same as the direction of the "Separate Legs-Right", that is 30° to the right. Meanwhile, keep the head, neck and waist upright; sink the shoulders and elbows; do not bend the upper

body forward or bow the head.

23. 左分腳

（1）重心後移，右腳尖外撇，上體右轉。兩拳變掌向左右分開，掌心均向外，眼看左手（圖2-128）。

（23）Separate Feet-Left

a. Shift the weight backward, swinging the right toes outward. Turn the upper body to the right. Then separate both hands, the right one going to the right front, the left one going to the left, both palms facing outward. Eyes look at the left hand (Figure 2-128).

圖2-127　　圖2-128

（2）重心前移至右腿，左腳收於右腳內側，上體微左轉。兩掌從左右兩側向下向內畫弧至腹前相交再舉抱於胸前，左掌在外，掌心均向內，眼看左前方（圖2-129）。

b. Shift the weight onto the right leg. Bring back the left foot and place it beside the right foot. Turn the upper body to the left. Both hands draw arcs inward to form an "X" in front of the abdomen and then raise them to the chest level. The left hand is on the outside of the right one, both palms facing the body. Eyes look at the left front (Figure 2-129).

（3）右腿微屈站穩，左腿屈膝提起，左腳尖向左前上方慢慢踢出，腳面展平，高過腰部。兩掌向左前和右方畫弧分開，掌心均向外，腕高與肩平，兩臂撐舉，肘關節微屈，左臂與左腿上下相對，眼看左手（圖2-130）。

c. Bend the right leg and stand on it firmly. Bend the left knee at the waist level and kick to the left front slowly with the toes, stretching the foot. Move both hands to the sides of the body, palms facing outward at the shoulder level. Arms are arched; elbows are bent. The left arm is above the left leg. Eyes look at the left hand (Figure 2-130).

【要領】

（1）此勢重心移動先後再前，後移兩手分，前移兩手相交叉成丁步，上下肢與身法要協調配合。

（2）分腳動作沉肩，鬆胯，兩肘墜，兩手撐，保持上體正直，頭頂，呼氣。

Key Points

（1）When shifting the weight backward, separate the two hands. When shifting the weight forward, cross the hands and form a T–Step. The limbs are coordinated with the body.

（2）When kicking, sink the shoulders and elbows; relax the hips; push the hands outward; maintain the upper body upright; draw the head up; breathe naturally.

圖2-129　　　　　　　圖2-130

24. 轉身拍腳

（1）左腿屈膝下落，身體以右腳掌為軸，順勢向右後轉身，左腳尖隨體轉內扣落地。兩掌從兩側向腹前畫弧下落，前臂外旋，掌心斜相對，頭隨身轉動（圖2-131）。

(24) Turn Around and Pat on the Foot

a. Bending the left leg, foot falls down. Pivot on the right forefoot, turning the upper body to the right, swinging the left toes inward and placing them onto the ground. Meanwhile, move both hands down to the lower abdomen to form "X". Rotate both arms outward, palms facing each other. The head follows the body (Figure 2-131).

（2）重心左移於左腿，身體繼續右後轉（側對上勢左分腳方向），右腳隨之轉正，腳尖點地。兩掌交叉相抱於胸前，右掌在外，掌心均向裏，眼看右前方（圖2-132）。

b. Shift the weight to the left leg. Continue to turn the upper body to the right. Right toes touch the ground and point forward. Both hands make an "X" in front of the chest. The left hand is on the inside, the right outside. Both palms face the body. Eyes look at the right front (Figure 2-132).

（3）左腿支撐，右腳向上踢擺，腳面展平。兩前臂內旋，掌心向外，右掌向前迎擊拍右腳面，高與頭齊；左掌向後畫弧分開，平舉於身體左方，腕高與肩平，眼看右手（圖2-133）。

c. The left leg support the weight. Lick upward with the right foot. Rotate both forearms and turn the palms facing outward. The right palm pats on the right foot at head level. The left hand draws an arc to the back and stops at the left side of the body at shoulder level. Eyes look at the right hand (Figure 2-133).

【要領】

（1）左腿屈膝、上體右後轉時，要注意兩胯相

圖2-131　　圖2-132　　圖2-133

合，重心微下蹲。

（2）擊拍時，繃腳抖腕，擊響於擺踢的最高點。
同時，要頂頭、立腰，兩腿均要自然伸直，呼氣配合。

Key Points

（1）When bending the left knee and turning the upper
body, pull the hips in; lower the weight.

（2）When patting on the foot, deliver the force to the foot
and hand; make a sound on the highest point; draw the head
up; straighten the waist; extend both legs naturally; breathe.

25. 進步栽捶

（1）左腿屈膝，右腿屈收，右腳前落，腳尖外
撇，上體右轉，重心前移。兩前臂外旋，左掌向上向
右畫弧，掌心轉向右；右掌翻轉下落至腰間，掌心向
上，頭隨上體右轉（圖2-134）。

(25) Step Forward and Punch Downward

a. Bend the left knee. Bring the right leg in and it steps
forward, swinging the toes outward. Shift the weight forward
and turn the upper body to the right. Rotate both forearms outward.
The left hand draws an arc to the upper right and turns over to
face right. The right hand turns over and falls down to the right
side of the waist, palm facing up. The head follows the body to
turn to the right (Figure 2-134).

（2）左腳向前上一步，腳跟著地，上體微左轉。右掌向右向上畫弧，屈肘握拳收於右耳側，拳心向下，左掌向下畫弧落於腹前，眼看前下方（圖2-135）。

b. The left foot steps forward with only the heel touching the ground. Turn the upper body to the left slightly. The right hand draws an arc to the upper right, bending the elbow and turning the right hand into a fist beside the right ear, palm facing down. The left hand draws an arc and falls in front of the abdomen. Eyes watch lower front (Figure 2-135).

（3）上體繼續左轉，稍向前俯身，重心前移成左弓步。右拳向前下方打出，高與腹平，拳面向前下

圖2-134　　　　　　　圖2-135

方，拳眼向左；左掌自左膝上方摟過，按於左胯旁，眼看右手（圖2-136）。

c. Continue to turn the upper body to the left. Bend the upper body forward slightly. Shift the weight forward to form a left Bow Step. Meanwhile, the right fist punches downward in front of the body. The palm faces the body, the eye of the fist facing left. Move the left hand around the left knee and stop it beside the left hip. Eyes watch the right hand (Figure 2–136).

【要領】

（1）拍腳後，右腳要先屈收再向前落步。

（2）左弓步與摟手栽拳要同時完成，栽拳方向

圖2-136　　　　　　圖2-137

為正前。

（3）栽拳時上體前傾約30°，須保持頂頭直腰，斜中寓正。

Key Points

（1）Bring the right foot in first, then take a step forward.

（2）Making the left Bow Step is at the same time as the punch.

（3）When punching downward, bend the upper body 30 forward; Draw the head and waist up and straight.

26. 斜飛勢

（1）重心後移，左腳尖外撇，上體左轉。右拳變掌向上向右畫弧，左掌向左畫弧，兩掌分開（圖2-137）。

(26) Diagonal Flight

a. Shift the weight backward. Swing the left toes outward. Turn the upper body to the left. Turn the right fist into an open palm which is facing upward. Move the right hand to the right in an arc. The left hand draws an arc to the left to separate the hands (Figure 2-137).

（2）重心前移，右腳收於左腳內側。左掌向上向右畫弧，屈臂於胸前，掌心斜向下；右掌向下向左畫弧，屈臂於腹前，掌心斜向上，兩臂交叉相抱，左前臂在上，眼看左手（圖2-138）。

b. Shift the weight forward. Bring the right foot in and place it beside the left foot. The left hand draws an arc to the upper right, the arm bent in front of the chest, palm facing downward diagonally. The right hand draws an arc downward first then to the left, palm facing up diagonally, arm bent in front of the abdomen. Both arms form an "X", the left arm above the right one. Eyes look at the left hand (Figure 2–138).

（3）上體微右轉，右腳向右側開步，腳跟著地，眼看左手（圖2-139）。

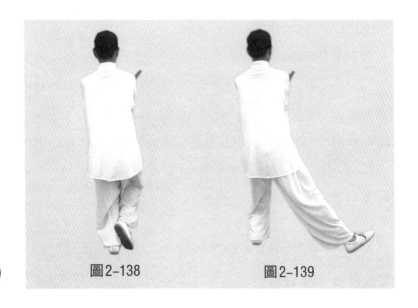

圖2-138　　　　　圖2-139

c. Turn the upper body to the right slightly. The right foot steps to the right, with only the heel touching the ground. Eyes look at the left hand (Figure 2–139).

（4）重心右移，上體左轉，右腿屈膝成右側弓步（橫襠步）。右肩向右傾靠，兩掌分別向右前上方和左前下方撐開，右掌略高於頭，掌心斜向上，左掌和胯同高，掌心斜向下，眼看左手（圖2-140）。

d. Shift the weight to the right. Turn the upper body to the left. Bend the right knee to form a right Side Bow Step. Meanwhile, the right shoulder leans to the right. Move the right hand to the right back, higher than the head, palm facing up-

圖2-140

ward diagonally. Move the left hand to the left front and stop it at waist level, palm facing downward diagonally. Eyes look at the left hand (Figure 2-140).

【要領】

（1）此勢動作選自吳氏太極拳，分靠時上體向右傾斜，要保持頂頭、立腰，斜中寓正。

（2）右腳落點要略後於左腳，不可成一條直線。

（3）兩掌分開時要有一種撐勁，沉胯，沉氣。

Key Points

（1）This movement is from Wu Style Taiji Quan. When the upper body is leaning to the right, keep the upper body and the waist steady and posture natural.

（2）Place the right foot behind the left one; do not place them on the same straight line.

（3）When the hands are separated, push them in opposite directions. Sink the hips. Sink the Energy (Qi).

27. 單鞭下勢

（1）重心左移，上體左轉，左腿屈膝，右腳跟稍外展。左掌變勾手，上提，腕與肩同高；右掌向左畫弧，經頭前擺至左肘內側，眼看右手（圖2-141）。

(27) Single Whip and push down the Body

a. Turn the upper body to the left. Shift the weight onto the left leg. Bend the left knee. The right toes are pointing the left front. Turn the left hand into a hook and raise it until the wrist is at shoulder-level. The right hand stops inside of the left elbow. Eyes look at the right hand (Figure 2–141).

（2）左腿全蹲，右腿鋪直，上體右轉，成右仆步。右掌下落經腹前順右腿內側向右穿出，掌心由內轉向外，指尖向右，眼看右手（圖2-142）。

b. Squat with the left leg and stretch the right leg straight to form a right "Crouch Stance". Turn the upper body to the

圖2-142

圖2-141

right. The right hand thrusts downward, past the abdomen, along the inside of the right leg. Rotate the palm outward, fingers pointing to the right. Eyes look at the right hand (Figure 2–142).

【要領】

（1）仆步時，上體要保持基本豎直，上體可略向前俯，做到儘量收髖、豎脊、頂頭，不要凸臀、低頭彎腰。

（2）仆步時，兩腳要全腳著地，不可掀腳，右腿要平鋪伸直，不可屈膝。

Key Points

（1）When squatting with the right leg, the upper body leans forward slightly. Both feet are placed on the ground firmly; keep spine upright; draw the head up; do not push the buttock out, or bow the head.

（2）When squatting with the right leg, both feet are entirely placed on the groud. Don't bend the right leg.

28. 金雞獨立（二）

（1）重心右移，上體右轉，右腳尖外展，左腳尖內扣，右腿屈膝前弓，左腿自然蹬直。右掌向上挑至體前，成側立掌，腕高與肩平；左臂內旋下落至身後，勾尖轉向上，眼看右掌（圖2–143）。

(28) Stands on One Leg (2)

a. Shift the weight to the right and turn the upper body to the right. Swing the right toes outward, left toes inward. Bend the right knee and extend the left leg. Raise the right hand in front of the body, palm facing left, fingers pointing up, and wrist at shoulder level. Rotate the left arm down to the back of the body, the hook pointing up. Eyes look at the right hand (Figure 2–143).

（2）重心前移，上體右轉，重心移於右腿，左腿屈膝向前上提起，腳尖下垂，右腿微屈站穩，成右獨立步。左勾手變掌，經體側向前向上挑起成側立

圖2-143

掌，指尖高與眉齊，右掌翻轉下按於右胯旁，眼看左手（圖2-144）。

b. Shift the weight forward and turn the upper body to the right. Shift the weight onto the right leg. Bend the left knee and lift it in front of the body, toes pointing down. Bend the right knee and stand on it firmly to form a right Independent Step. Change the left hand into an open palm and move it from the right to the upper front and stop it above the right leg at nose-level, palm facing left, elbow above the right knee. The right hand falls slowly to the outside the left hip, palm facing downward. Eyes look at the left hand (Figure 2-144).

（3）右腿稍屈，左腳落於右腳內側略後，重心移於左腿；上體左轉，右腿屈膝提起，腳尖下垂，左腿微屈站穩，成左獨立步。左掌翻轉按於左胯旁，右掌成側立掌挑至體前，指尖高與眉齊，眼看右手（圖2-145）。

c. Bend the right leg slightly. Place the left foot beside the right foot. Shift the weight onto the left leg and turn the upper body to the left. Lift the right leg, toes pointing down. Bend and stand on the left leg firmly to form an "Independent Step". Meanwhile, the left hand presses down to the outside of the left hip. Raise the right hand in front of the body at nose level, palm facing up. Eyes look at the right hand（Figure 2–145）.

【要領】

（1）重心站穩再提膝、挑掌、按掌，三個動作要協調配合，不可支離割裂。

（2）上體保持正直，注意鬆胯、沉肩；挑掌與按掌要上下對撐。

Key Points

（1）After standing firmly on the left leg, raise the right hand and press the left hand. The motions are coordinated.

（2）Keep the upper body upright and steady. Relax the hips and sink the shoulders. The force of both hands goes to op–

圖2-144　　　　　　　　　圖2-145

posite directions.

29. 退步穿掌

左腿稍屈，右腳後撤一步，右腿自然蹬直，左腿屈弓，左腳以前腳掌為軸順勢扭正，成左弓步。左臂外旋，左掌掌心翻轉向上，收經腰間，從右前臂上穿出，腕高與肩平；右臂內旋，橫掌下按於左肘下方，眼看左手（圖2-146）。

29. Withdraw Step and Thrust Left Palm

Bend the left knee slightly. The right foot takes a step backward. Bend the left leg. Pivot on the left forefoot to make the toes face forward and form a left Bow Step. Rotate the left arm outward, turning the palm to face up and bringing it at the left side of the waist. The left hand thrusts above the right fore-arm, wrist at shoulder level. Rotate the right arm inward and press down to the beneath of the left elbow, fingers pointing left. Eyes look at the left hand (Figure 2-146).

【要領】

（1）左腿屈膝，重心下降時，上體要保持正直。

（2）右腳後撤，左掌穿、右掌按與成左弓步要協調一致，同時完成。右掌要按於左肘下，不宜靠前或過後。

Key Points

（1）When bending the left and lowering the weight, keep upper body upright.

（2）The hand thrusts in coordination with the motions of the leg and the waist. The right palm should be right under the left elbow.

第四組

30. 虛步壓掌

（1）重心後移，上體右後轉，左腳尖內扣。右掌收至腹前，左掌舉於左額側上方，眼隨轉體平視（圖2-147）。

圖2-146   圖2-147

Group 4

(30) Empty Step and Press Palm

a. Shift the weight backward. Turn the upper body to the right. Swing the left toes inward. Bring the right hand in front of the abdomen. Raise the left hand above the left forehead. Eyes follow the body to look straight ahead (Figure 2-147).

（2）重心移於左腿，右腳提起，腳尖轉向前方，腳前掌落地，成右虛步。上體向下鬆沉，微向前俯，左掌自上而下橫按於右膝前上方，指尖向右；右掌按於右胯旁，指尖向前，眼看前下方（圖2-148）。

b. Shift the weight onto the left leg. Raise the right foot with the toes pointing forward and place the forefoot on the ground to form a right Empty Step. Lower the upper body and bend it forward slightly. The left hand press down in front of the right knee, fingers pointing right. The right hand goes to the outside of the right hip, fingers pointing forward. Eyes look at lower front(Figure 2-148).

【要領】

（1）完成動作時，上體向下鬆沉，胯下坐。

（2）虛步勁力前三後七，眼要看前下方。

Key Points

（1）When the movement is completed, sink and relax the body; sink the hips.

（2）For the Empty Step, the front leg supports 30% of the body; the rear one supports 70%. Eyes look at lower front.

31. 獨立托掌

左腳用力下踩，左腿微屈站穩，右腿屈膝提起，腳尖下垂，成左獨立步。右掌翻轉上托，舉於體前，掌心向上，腕高與胸平；左掌向左向上畫弧，撐於體側，腕高與肩平，掌心向外，指尖斜向上，眼看右手（圖2-149）。

圖2-148　　　　　　圖2-149

(31) Lift a Leg and a Palm

The left foot pushing the ground, stand on the left leg firmly with it bent slightly. Lift the right leg and bend it, toes pointing down to form a left Independent Step. Lift the right palm in front of the body, palm facing up, and wrist at chest level. The left palm draws an arc to the upper left and the arm is arched at the left side of the body, wrist at shoulder level, palm facing outward, fingers pointing up diagonally. Eyes look at right hand (Figure 2-149).

【要領】

（1）左腿慢慢伸直支撐，同時右腿屈膝提起，與托掌、撐掌協調一致，同時完成。

（2）右掌掌跟用力上托，左掌跟用力外撐，上體要正直，頂頭，鬆胯，氣下沉。

Key Points

（1）Extend the left leg slowly to support the body. Bend the right leg in coordination with the hands, moving and finish them at the same time.

（2）Deliver the energy to the bases of both palms. The torso is upright; draw the head up; relax the hips; Breathe through the abdomen.

32. 馬步靠

（1）上體微右轉，右腳前落，腳尖斜向右前方，重心移於右腳。右臂內旋，右掌翻轉下捋；左臂外旋，左掌向上向右畫弧，眼看前方（圖2-150）。

（32）Left Shoulder Strikes with Horse Stance

a. Turn the upper body to the right. The right foot falls down with the toes pointing the right front. Shift the weight to the right leg. Rotate the right arm inward and turn over the palm to pull downward. Rotate the left arm outward and draw an arc to the upper right. Eyes look ahead（Figure 2–150）.

（2）左腳收於右腳內側，上體繼續右轉。右掌

圖2-150

翻轉向上並向右畫弧舉於體側，高與頭平；左掌握拳，落於右腹前，拳心向下，拳眼向內，眼看右拳（圖2-151）。

b. Bring the left foot beside the right foot. Continue to turn the upper body to the right. Turn over the right palm to face up and draw an arc to the right side of the body at head level. Turn the left hand into a fist and it falls down in front of the abdomen, palm facing downward, the eye of the fist facing the body. Eyes look at right hand (Figure 2-151).

（3）上體左轉，左腳向左前方上步，重心略向前移，成半馬步。左臂內旋，擺至身體左側，向前靠出，左拳拳眼向內，拳面向下，置於左膝前；右掌屈收，經耳側推助左臂向前擠靠，掌心向左，掌指附於左上臂內側下端，眼看左前方（圖2-152）。

c. Turn the upper body to the left. The left foot takes a half step forward and shift the weight forward slightly to form a half Horse Step. Rotate the left arm inward and push it to the left front at the left side of the body, the eye of the left fist facing the body, palm facing outward in front of the left knee. Simultaneously, bend the right arm and push it from the right ear to the left. The right hand attaches on the inside of the left arm to help the force, palm facing left, fingers at the upper arm and near the elbow. Eyes look at right front（Figure 2-152）.

【要領】

（1）馬步靠下肢為半馬步，兩腳成丁字形，重心偏右腿。

（2）擠靠時上體下沉，圓襠，右手擠按左臂，形成左肩臂向左前方擠靠勁，同時要呼氣助力。

Key Points

（1）When squatting with the legs forming a half Horse Step, the feet form a T-shape; the weight is mostly on the right leg.

（2）When push both arms out, sink the body; the crotch of the legs is arched; the right hand presses the left arm to help the

圖2-151　　　　　　　　圖2-152

left shoulder push to the left front, exhale to increase the force.

33. 轉身大将

（1）重心後移，左腳尖外撇抬起。左拳變掌，左臂外旋，右臂內旋，兩掌心同時轉向外，並微向後收帶，眼看兩手（圖2-153）。

(33) Turn Body and Pull

a. Shift the weight backward. Raise the left toes and swing it outward. Rotate the left arm outward and turn the fist into an open palm. Rotate the right arm inward. Turn both palms outward and bring them back slightly. Eyes look at both hands (Figure 2-153).

（2）上體左轉，重心移向左腿，右腳收於左腳內側，兩腳平行向前，重心仍偏於右腿，並稍向上升高。左臂內旋屈肘橫掌提至胸前，掌心向外；右臂外旋，舉於身體右側，高與肩平，掌心斜向上，眼看右手（圖2-154）。

b. Turn the upper body to the left and shift the weight to the left leg. Bring the right foot beside the left foot to make them parallel with each other, toes pointing forward. The weight is mostly on the right leg and rises slightly. Rotate the left arm inward and bend the arm in front of the chest, palm facing outward, fingers pointing right. Rotate the right arm outward to the right side of the body at shoulder level, palm facing upward diagonally. Eyes look at right hand (Figure 2–154).

（3）以右腳前掌為軸，腳跟外展，身體左轉，右腿屈膝下蹲；左腳後撤一步，腳尖外展落地。兩掌隨轉體向左平捋至體前，右掌高與頭平，左掌置於右肘內側，兩掌心斜相對，眼看右掌（圖2–155）。

c. Pivot on the right forefoot and swing the heel outward. Turn the upper body to the left. Bend the right knee in a half squat. The left foot steps backward, swinging the toes outward and placing it on the ground. Both hands follow the body to pull in front of the body, the right palm at the head level, the

圖2-153　　　　圖2-154

left palm at the inside of the right elbow, both palms facing inward. Eyes look at right hand（Figure 2-155）.

（4）上體繼續左轉，重心左移，右腳跟外展，右
腿自然蹬直，左膝屈弓，成左側弓步（橫襠步）。兩掌
向左平捋的同時逐漸握拳，左臂外旋，左拳向左弧形捲
收於左腰間，拳心向上；右臂屈肘外旋滾壓置於體前，
右拳高與胸齊，拳心斜向上，眼看右拳（圖2-156）。

d. Continue to turn the upper body to the left and shift the
weight to the left. Swing the right heel outward, extend the
right leg and bend the left knee to form a left Bow Step. while
pulling the hands to the left, turn them into fists. Move the left

圖2-155　　　　　　　　　　圖2-156

fist to the left side of the waist, palm facing up. Rotate the right arm outward and press it down in front of the body, at chest level, palm facing upward diagonally. Eyes look at right hand (Figure 2–156).

【要領】

（1）兩掌挒時要與轉身配合，以身帶臂。

（2）重心左移成左側弓步與轉身壓拳同時進行。

（3）壓拳時力點在右前臂，上體要下沉落胯，前壓後拉，形成對拉勁，同時要呼氣助力。

Key Points

（1）Pull hands in coordination with the body; the body leads the arms.

（2）While the weight is shifting, form the Bow Step and press the fists down.

（3）When pressing the fists down, deliver the force to the right forearm. Lower the upper body and sink the hips; push the back backward; breathe to help the force.

34.歇步擒打

（1）上體右轉，重心右移。右臂內旋，屈肘上撐，右拳置於右額前，拳心向外；左臂內旋，左拳從身體左後方貼左腿穿出，拳心向後，眼看前方（圖2–

157）。

(34) Capture and Punch in low Squat with Crossing Legs

a. Turn the upper body to the right and shift the weight to the right. Rotate the right arm inward and bend the elbow upward. The fist stops in front of the right forehead, palm facing outward. Rotate the left arm inward and the fist thrusts along the left leg from the left back of the body, palm facing the back. Eyes look at the front (Figure 2–157).

（2）上體左轉，左腳尖外展，重心前移。右拳經體側下落捲收於右腰間，拳心向上；左拳變掌，向

圖2-157

前畫弧，掌心翻轉向右，頭隨體轉，眼看前方（圖2-158）。

b. Turn the upper body to the left. Swing the left toes outward. Shift the weight forward. The right fist falls to the right side of the waist, palm facing upward. Turn the left fist into an open palm and draw an arc forward, turning the palm to face right. The head follows the body. Eyes look at the front（Figure 2-158）.

（3）右腳經左腳前向左前方蓋步橫落，兩腿交叉屈蹲成歇步。左掌握拳，收於腹前，拳心向下，拳眼向內；右拳經左前臂上向前向下方打出，高與腹平，拳心向上，眼看右拳（圖2-159）。

圖2-158　　　　　圖2-159

c. The right foot steps in front of the left foot and form 90° to it. Cross the two legs and squat low. Turn the left palm into a fist and bring it in front of the abdomen, palm facing downward, the eye of the fist facing the body. The right fist punches to the lower front over the left forearm at the abdomen level, palm facing upward. Eyes look at the right fist (Figure 2-159).

【要領】

（1）左拳經身體左後方穿出時要貼於左腿，以上體向左前進身，催左肩、左肘、左拳節節前穿。

（2）成歇步時，後膝應頂住前膝窩，兩膝靠緊。

（3）擒打時，左拳在右前臂靠近右肘下方。

Key Points

（1）When the left fist is thrusting along the left leg, try to be close to the leg. Move the upper body to the left to push the left shoulder, elbow and the fist forward.

（2）When squatting with the crossing leg, the knee inside should touch the other knee outside.

（3）When the right fist is punching out, the left fist is under the right elbow.

35. 穿掌下勢

（1）身體慢慢上升，上體右轉，同時左腳收至右腳內側。兩拳變掌，右臂內旋，掌心翻轉向外，掌指向左，提至胸前；左臂外旋，掌心翻轉向外，掌指向左，舉至身體左側，眼看左手（圖2-160）。

(35) Thrust Palm and Push down the Body

a. Raise the body up slowly. Turn the upper body to the right. Meanwhile, bring the left foot beside the right foot. Turn both fists into open palms. Rotate the right arm inward and turn the palm facing outward, fingers pointing left at chest level. Rotate the left arm outward and turn the palm facing outward at the left side of the body, fingers pointing left. Eyes look at the left hand (Figure 2–160).

圖2-160

（2）上體右轉，右腿屈膝下蹲，左腿向左側伸出。兩掌向上向右畫弧，經面前擺至身體右側，掌心轉向斜下，指尖斜向右上，右掌伸舉於右前方，高與頭平；左掌屈臂擺至右肩前，高與肩平，眼看右手（圖2-161）。

b. Turn the upper body to the right. Bend the right leg in a squat. Extend the left leg to the left. Both hands draw arcs to the upper right, past in front of the face to the right side of the body, palms facing downward diagonally, fingers pointing the right front diagonally at head level. Move the left hand in front of the right shoulder. Eyes look at the right hand (Figure 2-161).

（3）右腿全蹲，左腿鋪直，上體左轉，成左仆步。兩掌繞轉，指尖轉向左，經腹前順左腿內側向前穿出，左掌在前，掌心向外；右掌在後，掌心向內，眼看左掌（圖2-162）。

c. Squat with the right leg and stretch the left leg straight, turning the upper body to the left to form a "Crouch Step". Both hands follow the body, fingers pointing the left, and then move down along the left leg. The left palm is ahead of the right palm. The left palm is facing outward, the right palm facing inward. Eyes look at the left hand (Figure 2-162).

【要領】

（1）仆步時，右腿要全蹲，左腿要平鋪伸直，不可屈膝。兩腳平行或稍外展，全腳著地踏實，上體略前俯，要收髖，坐胯，豎脊，頂頭。

（2）穿掌時，兩臂應屈肘，以指尖領先順左腿前穿，不可低頭彎腰。

Key Points

（1）When squatting with the right leg, stretch the left leg straight; do not bend it. Keep the feet parallel or swing the right toes a little bit outward. Both feet are placed on the ground firmly. The upper body should not lean forward too much. Pull the hips in. Keep the spine upright. Draw the head up.

圖2-161　　　　　　圖2-162

(2) When the hands are thrusting, bend both arms, led by finger, and move along the left leg; do not bow the head or waist.

36. 上步七星

（1）重心前移，上體左轉，左腳尖外撇，右腳尖內扣，右腿蹬直，左腿前弓。左掌向前向上挑起，腕高與肩平，掌心向右，指尖斜向上；右掌微向後拉，側置於右胯旁，眼看左掌（圖2-163）。

(36) Step up to Form the Seven Stars

a. Shift the weight forward and turn the upper body to the left. Swing the left toes inward. Extend the right leg and bend the left leg forward to form a left Bow Step. Meanwhile, raise the left hand with the wrist at shoulder level, palm facing right, fingers pointing up. Pull the right hand backward slightly and place it beside the right hip. Eyes look at the left hand (Figure 2-163).

（2）重心移於左腿，右腳向前上一步，腳前掌著地，成右虛步。左掌握拳，微向內收，拳心向內；右掌變拳向前向上架起，拳心向外，兩腕交疊，兩拳交叉於身前，高與肩平，右拳在外，兩臂撐圓，眼看左拳（圖2-164）。

b. Shift the weight onto the left leg. The right foot takes a step forward with only the forefoot touching the ground to form a right Empty Step. Meanwhile, the right hand draws an arc downward and forward. Change both hands to fists and let them meet in front of the body to form an "X" at shoulder level. The right fist is on the outside, palm facing outward. The left fist is on the inside, palm facing the body. Eyes look at the left fist (Figure 2–164).

【要領】

（1）左腿支撐要平穩，右腳上步和右拳前架要同時完成。

圖2-163　　　　圖2-164

（2）成虛步時，兩腿均要屈曲，不可站直，肩胯要鬆沉。

Key Points

（1）The left leg supports the body steadily. The stepping forward and the raising of both fists are finished at the same time.

（2）When forming the right Empty Step, bend both legs; do not stand straight. Relax and sink the hips and shoulders.

37. 退步跨虎

（1）右腳向右後方撤一步，重心後移至右腿，上體右轉。右拳變掌向右下方畫弧至右胯旁，掌心向下；左拳同時變掌，隨身體右轉稍向右畫弧，掌心向右，頭稍右轉，眼看右前方（圖2-165）。

(37) Step Back to Ride a Tiger

a. The right foot takes a step backward. Shift the weight onto the right leg and turn the upper body to the right. Turn the right fist into an open palm and move it to the lower right in an arc until it is beside the right hip, palm facing down. The left fist turns into an open palm and draw an arc to the right, palm facing right. Turn the head to the right slightly. Eyes look at the right front (Figure 2-165).

（2）左腳稍向後收，腳前掌著地於右腳前，上

體左轉，身體略向下屈蹲。右掌向上畫弧經頭前再向
左向下畫弧，落於左大腿外側，掌心向外；左手經胸
前畫弧下落於左胯側，掌心向下。眼隨身轉，看右手
（圖2-166）。

b. Bring the left foot backward slightly and place the forefoot on the ground ahead of the right foot. Turn the upper body
to the left and lower the weight slightly. The right hand draws
an arc upward, past in front of the head, to the lower left and
stops outside the left leg, palm facing outward. The left hand
draws an arc downward to the outside of the left hip, palm facing downward. Eyes follow the body to look at the right hand
(Figure 2-166).

圖2-165　　　　圖2-166

（3）右腳蹬地，獨立站穩；左腿前舉，膝微屈，腳面展平，腳尖稍內扣。右掌向前向上挑起成側立掌，腕高與肩平；左掌變勾手，同時上提舉於左方，高與肩平，屈腕，勾尖向下。上體左轉，眼看左前方（圖2-167）。

c. Stand on the right leg steadily. Lift the left leg forward, bending the knee slightly, extending the foot and toes pointing inward slightly. The right hand is raised as a Standing Hand, wrist at shoulder level. Turn the left hand into a hook and raise it in the left side of the body at shoulder level, the wrist bending, the hook pointing down. Turn the upper body to the left. Eyes look at the left front （Figure 2-167）.

【要領】

（1）提膝舉腿、勾手挑掌要同時完成，不可分割。

（2）完成時，要沉肩鬆胯，兩手對撐，右膝微屈站穩，左腳面要展平，腳尖不可勾蹺，眼要向左前方看。

Key Points

（1）Lift the hand and leg at the same time.

（2）When the movement is completed, sink the shoulders; relax the hips; push both hands outward; bend the right knee and stand on it steadily. Extend the left foot flatly; the toes should not point backward. Eyes look at the left front.

38.轉身擺蓮

（1）左腳前落，腳跟先著地，腳尖內扣，上體右轉。右臂內旋，右掌翻轉向下，屈肘向右平帶；左勾手變掌，掌心轉向上，自後向前平擺至體側。頭隨體轉，眼看前方（圖2-168）。

（38）Turn with Lotus Kick

a. The left foot steps forward, with the heel on the ground first, and then swing the toes inward. Turn the upper body to the right. Rotate the right arm inward to make the palm facing

圖2-167　　　　　　　　　圖2-168

downward, bending the elbow and moving it to the right. Change the left hand from the hook to an open palm and turn it over to face upward. Move it beside the body. The head follows the body. Eyes look ahead（Figure 2–168）.

（2）兩腳以前掌為軸，向右後轉體。左掌擺至體前，掌心向上，高與頭平；右掌翻轉向上，經胸前及左肘下方向左穿出。頭隨體轉，眼向前看（圖2–169）。

b. Pivot on both forefeet and turn the body 180° to the right. Move the left hand in front of the body, palm facing upward at head level. Turn the right hand over to face upward and thrust it forward from the left side of the waist over the upper side of the right wrist at eye level, fingers pointing upward diagonally. The right hand falls under the left elbow and faces downward. Eyes look at the front（Figure 2–169）.

（3）上體右轉不停，至與「上步七星」勢成背向，重心落於左腿，右腳尖虛點地。右掌穿出後向上向右畫弧，同時前臂內旋，掌心轉向右，指尖向上，置於身體右側，腕高與肩平；左掌自右臂內側翻轉下落，收於右肩前下方，掌心向右，眼看右手（圖2–170）。

c. Continue to turn the upper body to the right until it faces the opposite direction of the "Step up and Form Seven Stars". Shift the weight onto the left leg and lift the right heel. Move the right hand to the upper right in an arc. Meanwhile, rotate the arm inward until the palm faces right, fingers pointing upward, the fingers at the right side of the body, wrist at shoulder level. Turn the left hand over and it falls down to the lower front of the right shoulder, palm facing right. Eyes look at the right hand (Figure 2-170).

（4）右腳提起，向左向上向右做扇形外擺，腳面展平，上體左轉。兩掌自右向左平擺，在頭前先左

圖2-169   圖2-170

後右依次擊拍右腳面，眼看兩手（圖2-171）。

d. Lift the right leg and swing it from the left to the upper right, extending the foot naturally. Turn the upper body to the left. Move both hands to the left first, then across the head to the right and then to the left to pat on the right foot with the left hand first, then the right one. Eyes look at both hands (Figure 2-171).

【要領】

（1）擺蓮腳，動作要柔和連貫，手腳配合要協調一致，上體要正直，頂頭，立腰，沉肩，展臂，擊拍要兩響。

（2）擺腿要做扇形，重心平穩，動作不宜過快、過猛。

Key Points

（1）Move smoothly. Hands and feet are co-operated. Keep the body and waist upright. Draw the head up. Sink the shoulders. Extend the arms and pat the foot to make a sound with each hand.

（2）When the leg swinging, keep the weight steady; do not make a rush or sudden move.

39. 彎弓射虎

（1）右小腿屈收，右腿屈膝提於體前，腳尖下垂，左腿獨立站穩，上體左轉。兩掌繼續左擺，左掌擺至身體左側，右掌擺至左肩前下方，掌心均向下，高與肩平，眼看左掌（圖2-172）。

（39）Draw a Bow and Shoot the Tiger

a. Raise the right leg and bend the knee in front of the body, toes pointing downward. Stand on the left leg steadily. Turn the upper body to the left. Move both hands to the left, the right one to the lower front of the left shoulder, the left one to the left side of the body, palms facing downward at shoulder level. Eyes look at the left hand (Figure 2-172).

圖2-171　　　　　　圖2-172

（2）左腿屈膝下蹲，右腳向右前方落步，上體右轉。兩掌同時下落畫弧，眼看兩手（圖2-173）。

b. Bend the left knee in a half squat. The right foot steps to the right front.Turn the upper body to the right. Both hands draw arcs downward. Eyes look at both hands（Figure 2-173）.

（3）重心前移，上體右轉。兩掌向下向右畫弧至身體右側時兩掌握拳，拳心向下，眼看右拳（圖2-174）。

c. Shift the weight forward. Turn the upper body to the right. Both hands draw arcs downward, and then to the right; and change them into fists at the right side of the body, palm facing downward. Eyes look at the right fist（Figure 2-174）.

（4）上體左轉，右腿屈膝前弓，左腿自然伸直，成右弓步。左拳經面前向左前方打出，高與鼻平，拳心斜向下；右拳同時屈肘向左前方打出，至右額前，拳心向外，拳眼斜向下，眼看左拳（圖2-175）。

d. Turn the upper body to the left. Bend the right knee and extend the left leg to form a right Bow Step. The left fist passes the face to punch to the front left, palm facing the front left at nose height, palm facing downward diagonally. The right fist punches to the front left at right forehead, palm facing outward. Eyes look at the left fist (Figure 2–175).

【要領】

（1）落腳擺掌時，左腿要屈蹲，右腳慢慢落地，腳跟先著地，不可做成「砸夯」步。

（2）弓步轉身打拳動作要柔順，兩拳貫打時，鬆胯下沉，勁順脊背達於拳面。

Key Points

（1）When stepping, bend the left knee; place the right foot down slowly, with the heel on the ground first. Do not make heavy steps.

（2）When punching, relax and sink the hips. Deliver the

圖2-173　　圖2-174　　圖2-175

energy from the spine to the fists.

40. 左攬雀尾

（1）重心後移，右腳尖外撇抬起，上體右轉。兩拳變掌，左掌向左伸展，右掌翻轉向下畫弧至右腰間，掌心向上，頭隨身轉（圖2-176）。

(40) Grasp Bird's Tail – Left

a. Shift the weight backward. Swing the right toes outward and turn the upper body to the right. Change both fists into open palms. Extend the left arm to the left. The right hand draws an arc downward to the right side of the waist, palms facing up. The head follows the upper body to the right (Figure 2-176).

（2）重心前移至右腿，左腳收至右腳內側。右掌自下向右再翻轉向上畫弧，左掌由左向下畫弧，兩掌在胸前上下相抱，掌心相對，眼看右掌（圖2- 177）。

b. Shift the weight onto the right leg and bring the left foot beside the right foot. The right hand draws an arc to the right, and then turns over to move upward. The left hand draws an arc downward. Both hands are coordinated with each other as if holding a ball. Palms are facing each other. Eyes look at the right hand (Figure 2-177).

（3）上體下沉微右轉，左腳向前上步，腳跟著地，眼向前看（圖2-178）。

c. Lower the weight and turn the upper body to the right slightly. The left foot steps to the left front with only the heel on the ground Eyes look at the front (Figure 2-178).

（4）上體左轉，重心前移，左腿屈膝前弓，左腳踏實，右腿自然伸直，成左弓步。左前臂向前出，左掌心向內，高與肩平；右掌按落於右胯旁，掌心向下，眼看左手（圖2-179）。

d. Turn the upper body to the left. Shift the weight forward. Extend the right leg and bend the left knee to form a left Bow

圖2-176　　　圖2-177　　　圖2-178

Step. At the same time, the left arm pushes outward. The left wrist and forearm are at shoulder height, palm facing in. The right hand draws an arc downward to the right side of the hip, palm facing down. Eyes look at the left hand (Figure 2–179).

（5）上體微左轉，左掌稍向左前伸並翻轉掌心向下，右掌同時經腹前向前向左上畫弧，並翻轉使掌心向上置於右前臂內側下方，眼看左手（圖2-180）。

e. Turn the upper body to the left slightly. Extend the left hand forward and turn it over to face down. Turn over the right hand to face up, move it past the abdomen to the upper front and stop it under the left forearm. Eyes look the left hand (Fig-

圖2-179　　　　　圖2-180

ure 2–180）。

（6）上體右轉，重心後移，兩掌下捋，經腹前向右後上方畫弧至右掌，高與肩平，右掌掌心斜向前；左掌屈臂擺至右胸前，掌心向內，眼看右手（圖2–181）。

f. Turn the upper body to the right. Shift the weight backward. Both hands draw arcs past abdomen to right back until the right palm gets at shoulder level, palm facing the front diagonally. Bend the left arm in the right front of the chest, palm facing in. Eyes look at the right hand (Figure 2–181).

圖2–181

（7）上體左轉，面向前方。右掌屈臂捲收，掌指貼近左腕內側；左臂平屈胸前，左掌掌心向內，指尖向右，眼看前方（圖2-182）。

g. Turn the upper body to the left to face forward. Bend the right arm and place the hand close to the inside of the left wrist. Bend the left arm horizontally in front of the chest, palm facing in, fingers pointing to the right. Eyes look at the front (Figure 2-182).

（8）重心前移，成左弓步。雙臂向前擠出，兩臂撐圓，右掌指附於左腕內側，高與肩平，眼看左前臂（圖2-183）。

h. Shift the weight forward. Bend the right knee and extend

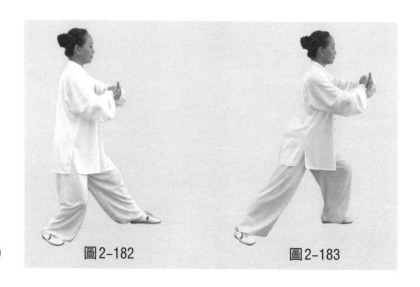

圖2-182　　　　　圖2-183

the left leg to form a left Bow Step. Push both hands forward at shoulder level, arms rounded. The right hand is still at the inside of the left wrist. Eyes look at the left forearm (Figure 2–183).

（9）兩掌內旋，右掌經左掌上伸出，兩掌分開，與肩同寬，掌心均向下，眼看前方（圖2–184）。

i. Rotate both arms inward. Extend the right arm forward over the left palm and separate the hands apart to the shoulder width, palms facing forward, fingers pointing up. Sink the wrists and relax the palms. Eyes look at the front (Figure 2–184).

（10）身體後坐，重心後移於右腿，左腳尖上蹺。兩臂屈肘，兩掌經胸前下落至腹前，掌心向前下

圖2–184

方，眼向前平視（圖2-185）。

j. Shift the upper body backward and shift the weight onto the right leg. Raise the left toes. Bend both arms and bring them in front of the chest then let them fall down to the abdomen, palms facing the lower front. Eyes look at the front (Figure 2-185).

（11）重心前移，成左弓步。兩掌平行向上向前按出，腕高與肩平，掌心向前，指尖向上，蹋腕舒掌，眼看前方（圖2-186）。

k. Shift the weight forward to form a left Bow Step. Push both hands to the upper front at shoulder level, palms facing forward, fingers pointing up. Eyes look at the front (Figure 2-186).

【要領】

（1）「攬雀尾」是掤、捋、擠、按四勢的總稱，做每個分動作的定勢時，肢體要膨脹，勁力要貫注，動作要沉穩，體現動作由虛到實的變化。在動作的連接上既要有虛實轉換，又要連續銜接，在節奏、勁力、意念上不可中斷。

（2）左臂掤時，用腰帶動左臂，左手像套火爐似的向前向上掤出，臂要撐圓，分手、鬆腰、弓腿三者協調一致。

（3）捋時，上體不可前傾、後仰、右歪，不可凸臀，下捋要隨腰轉，走弧線。左腳掌全腳著地，不可掀腳尖，眼要隨身向右後看右手。

（4）擠時，上體正直，擠手與鬆腰弓腿一致；兩手掌要有空隙，不可貼實；兩手前擠與脊背相對撐，兩肘不可上揚。

（5）按時兩手須走曲線；兩手回收時，上體不可後仰，兩肘下垂，不要外揚；前按時上體不可前傾，低頭；兩手相距要略窄於兩肩，兩臂要有一定曲度，兩肘垂沉，不可僵直。

Key Points

（1） The movement is combined by "Forearm Push

圖2-185　　　　　圖2-186

(Peng)", "Pulling with Two Hands (Lü)", "Pulling with Two Hands (Lü)", Pressing (An). When each movement is settled, the entire body is full of energy. Move steady, showing the transferring from the empty to the solid. Motions are connected smoothly at the speed, force, and mind with no pause.

(2) During practising "Forearm Push (Peng)", pay attention to using waist in leading the left arm and making it rounded. The hands separating, waist relaxing, and bow step making should be all coordinated.

(3) While practising "Pulling with Two Hands (Lü)", the upper body should not lean backward or outward. Do not pull buttock out. Both hands follow the waist to move in an arc. The right foot is entirely placed on the ground. Eyes are following the waist; turn head over to look at the right hand.

(4) While practising "Push with Arm and Hand", keep the upper body upright. The pushing hands, relaxing waist, and banding the leg are all coordinated. Place the right hand on the left one lightly; do not stick on it. As the hands push forward, pull the back backward; do not raise the elbows.

(5) While pressing, Both hands should be moved curvedly. When both hands are pulled back, the upper body should not bend backward. Sink the elbows; do not push them outward. Both hands are apart, narrower than the shoulder width.

Arms are curved, not rigid.

41. 十字手

（1）重心右移，上體右轉，左腳尖內扣，右腳尖外展。右掌隨身體右擺至面前，掌心向外；左掌分於身體左側，掌心亦向外，眼看右手（圖2-187）。

(41) Cross Hands

a. Shift the weight onto the right and turn the upper body to the right. Swing the left toes inward, right toes outward. The right hand follows the body to the right and stops in front of the face, palm facing outward. The left hand goes to the left side of the body, palm facing outward. Eyes look at the right hand (Figure 2-187).

圖2-187

（2）右腳尖繼續外展，重心右移，上體右轉不停，左腿自然蹬直。右掌擺至身體右側，兩掌左右平舉於身體兩側，兩肘略屈，掌心向前，眼隨右掌（圖2-188）。

b. Continue to swing the right toes outward and turn the upper body to the right. Shift the weight to the right. Extend the left leg. Move the right hand to the right side of the body. Raise both arms at shoulder level, bending arms, palm facing forward. Eyes look at the right hand（Figure 2-188）.

（3）重心左移，右腳尖內扣，上體左轉。兩掌向下向內畫弧，於腹前兩腕相交，兩掌合抱，舉至胸前，

圖2-188

右掌在外，掌心均向內，眼看兩掌（圖2-189）。

c. Shift the weight onto the left. Swing the right toes inward. Turn the upper body to the left. Both hands draw arcs downward simultaneously and meet in front of the abdomen to form an "X". The right hand is on the outside. Both palms face the body. Eyes look at the hands (Figure 2-189).

（4）右腳內收至兩腳與肩同寬落地，腳尖向前，成開立步；隨即上體轉正，兩腿慢慢直立。兩掌交叉成斜十字形抱於體前，掌心向內，高與肩平，眼看兩手（圖2-190）。

d. Bring the right foot close to the left foot with shoulder

圖2-189   圖2-190

width apart. Stand up slowly and the weight is shared by both feet. The feet are parallel to each other, toes pointing to the front. Meanwhile, both hands draw arcs downward simultaneously and meet in front of the chest to form an "X". The right hand is on the outside. The arms are arched with wrists at shoulder level, palms facing the body. Eyes look the hands (Figure 2-190).

【要領】

（1）轉體扣腳、弓腿、分手、合手要連貫銜接，不可有停頓。

（2）兩手在兩側畫弧下落時，不可低頭彎腰；收右腳時，保持上體正直，不可向左歪斜。

（3）兩手交叉相抱，要圓背、撐肘，肩部要放鬆，兩手腕距胸20公分左右。

（4）左右兩腳內扣要適度，保證兩腳平行，腳尖向正前。

Key Points

（1）The movement of the turning body, swinging foot, bending legs, and moving hands are connected smoothly without pause.

（2）When both hands draw arcs from both sides of the body, the upper body should not bow. When bringing the right foot to the left foot, maintain an upright upper body; do not move to the left or right.

(3) When both hands cross in front of the chest, both arms have to be arched; elbows rounded; shoulders relaxed; the wrists 20 cm down from the chest.

(4) Move the feet to be parallel, shoulder width apart, toes pointing forward.

42. 收 式

（1）兩前臂內旋，兩掌邊翻邊平行分開，與肩同寬，掌心向前下方，眼向前看（圖2-191）。

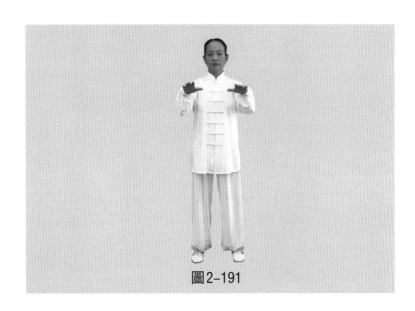

圖2-191

(42) Closing

a. Rotate both arms inward. Turn both hands outward and separate them to be shoulders' width apart. Hands are facing downward. Eyes look straight ahead (Figure 2–191).

（2）兩掌漸漸下落至腿外側，鬆肩垂臂，上體自然正直，眼向前看（圖2–192）。

b. Drop the arms slowly to the sides of the legs. The upper body is upright. Eyes look at straight ahead (Figure 2–192).

（3）左腳收至右腳旁，兩腳併攏，腳尖向前，身體自然直立，呼吸平穩均勻，眼看前方（圖2–193）。

圖2–192   圖2–193

c. Bring in the left foot gently and place it next to the right feet, toes facing forward. The upper body is upright. Breathe evenly. Eyes look at straight ahead（Figure 2-193）.

【要領】

（1）兩掌由交叉分開時，兩臂內旋應順勢向前翻轉兩手，不要折腕、上翻手指。

（2）兩臂下落時要沉肩、墜肘，屈臂帶動兩手回落，不要用勁下按。

（3）收式要鬆靜、沉穩，保持正常行拳均勻速度。

（4）完成全套動作後應略停片刻，不要匆忙走動。

Key Points

（1）When both hands are separating from the "X", both arms should be rotated inward. When turning over the hands, do not bend the wrists too much; do not bend fingers upwards.

（2）When the arms fall down, sink the shoulders and elbows. Bend the arms slightly to lead the hands down to the sides of the body. Do not be stiff.

（3）Keep calm and move with the same speed as other movements.

（4）After completing the full form, have a rest; do not rush to walk.

附 42式太極拳動作佈局路線圖

　　熟悉並掌握套路動作線路佈局變化十分重要，因為步法的變化，落腳之位置和方向，不僅影響套路演練的連貫性和美感，更重要的是它確保了每個招式的方向、位置和根基的穩固。

　　套路的練習目的不僅在於熟練動作，還包含了對肢體動作乃至招式之間的起承轉合的體悟，對於在攻防實踐中的運用招式有直接的影響，在增強表演觀賞效果方面也有重要的作用（見附圖）。

Appendix Path Map of the 42-form Taiji Quan Movements

It is important to understand the path of the TaiJi forms. The location, the direction, and the translation between the steps have a great impact on the coherence of the whole form. More important, the path provides a solid foundation for each movement. When practising, one should not only be familiar with the movements, but also understand the connection between the movements, which is more important when applying to attacking and defending (see the figure on Page 100).

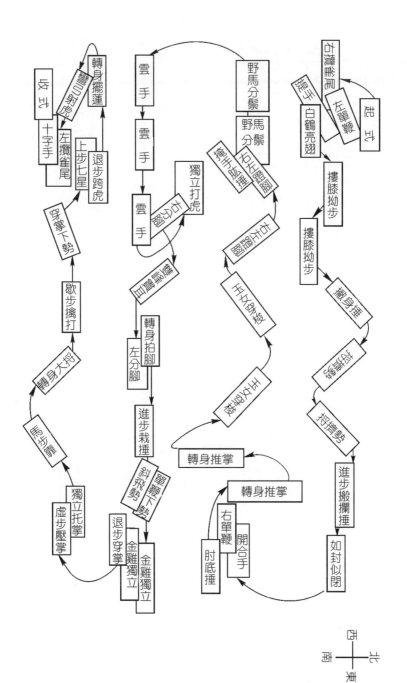

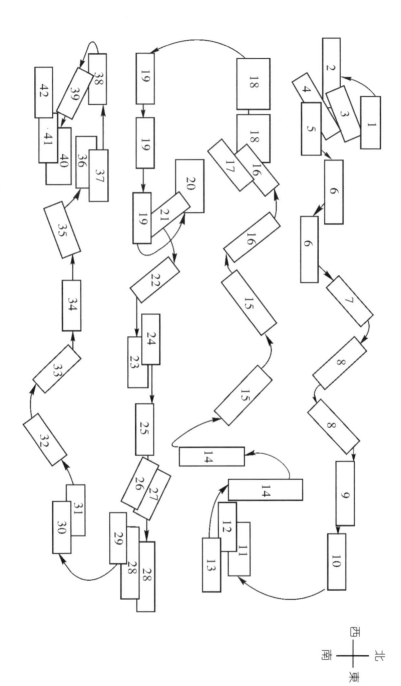

1. Opening

2. Grasp Bird's Tail – Right

3. Single Whip – Left

4. Lift Hand in Front of the Body

5. White Crane Spreads Wings

6. Brush Knees and Twist Steps（2）

7. Sidle and Punch

8. Pull and Press（2）

9. Step forward, Deflect, Parry and Punch

10. Withdraw and Push

11. Opening and Closing Hands

12. Single Whip – Right

13. Fist under the Elbow

14. Turn Body and Push（2）

15. Fair Lady Works at Shuttles（2）

16. Kick with the Heel – Right and Left（2）

17. Hide and Roll Arm Punch

18. Splitting Wild Horse's Mane（2）

19. Cloud Hands（3）

20. Stand on One Leg and Hit a Tiger

21. Separate Feet – Right

22. Strike Ears with Both Fists

23. Separate Feet – Left

42
式太極拳
學與練

歡迎至本公司購買書籍

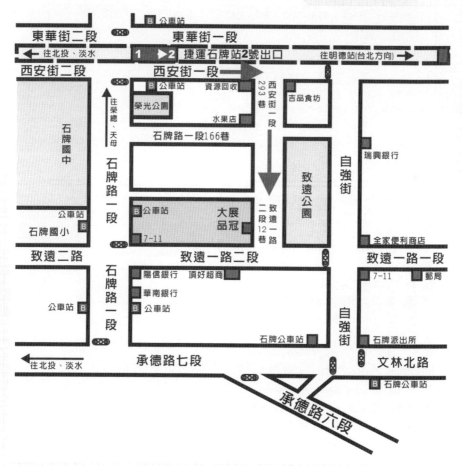

建議路線

1. 搭乘捷運・公車

　　淡水線石牌站下車，由石牌捷運站2號出口出站(出站後靠右邊)，沿著捷運高架往台北方向走(往明德站方向)，其街名為西安街，約走100公尺(勿超過紅綠燈)，由西安街一段293巷進來(巷口有一公車站牌，站名為自強街口)，本公司位於致遠公園對面。搭公車者請於石牌站(石牌派出所)下車，走進自強街，遇致遠路口左轉，右手邊第一條巷子即為本社位置。

2. 自行開車或騎車

　　由承德路接石牌路，看到陽信銀行右轉，此條即為致遠一路二段，在遇到自強街(紅綠燈)前的巷子(致遠公園)左轉，即可看到本公司招牌。

國家圖書館出版品預行編目資料

42式太極拳學與練 ／ 李壽堂　編著
　　——初版，——臺北市，大展，2014〔民103.10〕
　　　面；21公分 ——（中英文對照武學；2）
　　ISBN　978－986－346－042－8（平裝；附影音光碟）

1. 太極拳
528.972　　　　　　　　　　　　　　　　　103015600

42 式太極拳學與練 附 VCD

編　　著／李壽堂
校　　訂／張連友
責任編輯／王躍平　　張東黎
發 行 人／蔡森明
出 版 者／大展出版社有限公司
社　　址／台北市北投區（石牌）致遠一路2段12巷1號
電　　話／（02）28236031・28236033・28233123
傳　　眞／（02）28272069
郵政劃撥／01669551
網　　址／www.dah-jaan.com.tw
E－mail／service@dah-jaan.com.tw
登 記 證／局版臺業字第2171號
承 印 者／傳興印刷有限公司
裝　　訂／承安裝訂有限公司
排 版 者／弘益電腦排版有限公司
授 權 者／山西科學技術出版社
初版1刷／2014年（民103年）10月

定　價／300元

大展好書　好書大展
品嘗好書　冠群可期